If This Land Could Talk

◆

Homesteading on the Northern Plains

Judy R. Cook

*For Fay,
my good friend
and fellow alto.*

Judy Cook

iUniverse, Inc.
New York   Bloomington

Acclaim for *If This Land Could Talk*

"Wow! … Great job of bringing this man [Tom] and his times to life, mostly through the dialogue of his neighbors. I had the sense of sitting in a theater watching a movie about the Great Depression. I'd love to know how/where she dug up all the captivating detail. Definitely a winner!"
Megan Smolenyak Smolenyak, co-founder of RootsTelevision.com, author, and genealogical researcher.

"A well-researched account of history and personalities in early North Dakota."
Fred Bon, Kidder County farmer and businessman

"Like a beautiful quilt pieced together from beloved bits of fabric, this story of life on the Northern Plains has been written with reverence and compassion, and it too will warm generations to come."
Jennie Nash, author, *The Last Beach Bungalow*

"*If This Land Could Talk* evokes something rare and vital–a woman's deep love for her childhood home. Cook has composed a love song to the Northern Plains. She is a wonderful writer, and this is a terrific book."
Patricia Dunn M.A., M.F.T.

"Judy Cook has written a lovingly and thoroughly researched family saga with a cast full of wonderful characters."
Bruce Bauman, author, *And The Word Was*

Several book chapters won prizes in writing contests sponsored by Southwest Manuscripters, South Bay Cities Genealogical Society, and Southern California Genealogical Society.

In memory of my father. He lives on through his stories.

If This Land Could Talk

Homesteading on the Northern Plains

iUniverse books may be ordered through booksellers or by contacting:

iUniverse
1663 Liberty Drive
Bloomington, IN 47403
www.iuniverse.com
1-800-Authors (1-800-288-4677)

A version of "A Life's Work" was first published May/June 2001 in *The Searcher*, the journal of the Southern California Genealogical Society.

An excerpt from "Depression and War" was first published November 2004 in the Southwest Manuscripters journal, *The Write Stuff!*

ISBN: 978-0-595-48192-7 (pbk)
ISBN: 978-0-595-49997-7 (cloth)
ISBN: 978-0-595-60286-5 (ebk)

Printed in the United States of America

Contents

Acknowledgments

Thank you to all who helped me complete this labor of love. Primary contributors were Pearl Price Janke, Evelyn Shirley Price Giese, Dennis Price, and Dale Price. While they were still with us, I interviewed Melvin Shirley, Agnes Shirley Glock, Gilbert Shirley, Hilda Shirley Otto, Edna Shirley Shuford, Shirley Glock Bauer, Cecile Shirley, Vera Wetzel, and Mary White. I received additional information from interviews with James Otto, Darrell Wetzel, Fred Bon, Joyce Moores Olson, Kay Shirley, and Glen Shirley.

I am grateful for photos and documents from James Otto, Helen Stenberg White, Marvin Stenberg, Gloria Shirley Radtke, Dianne Janke Dronen, Thomas Janke, Allan Price, Everett Price, Polly Price Damaska, Velma Hanson Trautmann, Dorothy Erlanger Rich, Tom Swanson, Carrie Pardo, and Douglas Wick.

I am indebted to early readers Pat Dalby, Faye Schwartz, Darrell Wetzel, and Fred Bon, and to fellow writers Candy, Art, Vivian, Madonna, Jennie, Bruce, Pat, Leonia, and Kathy, to name a few.

Special thanks to my husband, Bob; my children, Brenda and Michael; and their spouses, Bryan and Tina, for their ongoing support. Bob digitized my photos and provided essential computer expertise. Thanks to my grandchildren, Lauren, Brandon, and Alex, for bringing me joy.

Foreword

Twenty years ago I published *North Dakota Place Names*, an effort that included traveling around the state visiting with countless old-timers who had lived their lives in North Dakota's smallest communities. The amazing life stories they told were fascinating, but beyond the scope of my book. *If This Land Could Talk* ensures that such stories are not lost.

Judy (Price) Cook, a longtime Californian who grew up on the prairies of Kidder County in central North Dakota, spent many childhood hours enthralled by the tales told by her elders. As an adult, she continued to press her relatives about the signature events of their lives. And best of all, Judy kept notes!

In the spirit of full disclosure, I must state that a few of the characters in this book are my relatives, too, although Judy and I are not related. That said, Judy accurately portrays the stories of typical North Dakotans who lived through some of the most amazing years in history. Most of the personalities have passed away, and sadly the same might soon be said for some of their communities.

Anyone interested in North Dakota history—or the saga of pioneers homesteading the American West—will find this book captivating. The characters in the book are real, as are the events described. Judy's flair for writing makes the book an easy read, and one that will be hard to put down.

Douglas A. Wick

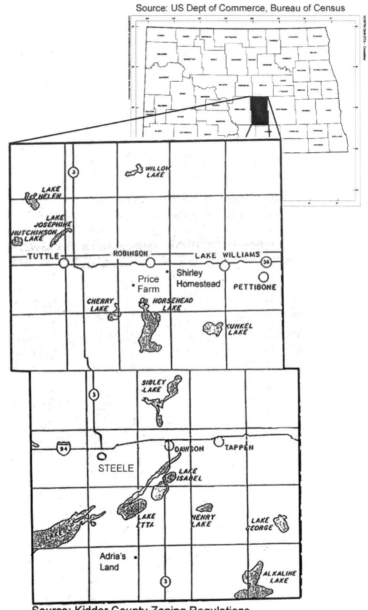

Source: Kidder County Zoning Regulations

Kidder County, North Dakota

Family Tree

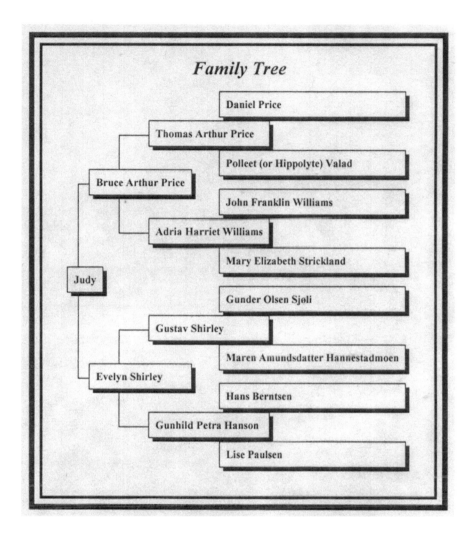

- Judy
  - Bruce Arthur Price
    - Thomas Arthur Price
      - Daniel Price
      - Polleet (or Hippolyte) Valad
    - Adria Harriet Williams
      - John Franklin Williams
      - Mary Elizabeth Strickland
  - Evelyn Shirley
    - Gustav Shirley
      - Gunder Olsen Sjøli
      - Maren Amundsdatter Hannestadmoen
    - Gunhild Petra Hanson
      - Hans Berntsen
      - Lise Paulsen

Author's Prologue

I have based this book on fact and family lore regarding the Dakota prairies during the early 1900s. Characters, dates, and places are real. Only a few minor characters are composite characters. Events described are true, depicted as I recalled them and filtered through my childhood memory, although all memories are imperfect.

During this project, I became hooked on genealogy. However, this book is not intended as a genealogical study with vital statistics. It is my family history, focusing on my four grandparents, who homesteaded in North Dakota, and the land that played a central role in their lives.

I came to know my grandparents through visits to homesteads, courthouses, churches, and cemeteries. I researched news accounts, public records, family photos and papers, and Internet records, and questioned countless family friends and relatives. Extensive interviews tapped into the unique recollections of my mother, Evelyn; my aunt, Pearl; and my brothers, Dennis and Dale. If documents conflicted with each other or people's memories, I used my best judgment to structure the story.

I deeply regret that I didn't know my paternal grandparents, Tom and Adria Price. My maternal grandmother, Petra Shirley, died when I was five, but Gust Shirley lived into my adulthood.

Since no diaries could be located, I constructed scenes and dialogue to dramatize my ancestors' lives using their habitual patterns of speech, manner, and dress. Sometimes, I assumed motivation from accumulated evidence.

My father, Bruce Price, died in 1990, before I began this labor of love. Yet as the family storyteller, his tales figure prominently in my memory. I was delighted to discover that my research validated his stories. When I inherited my father's photo album, the people pictured in it became an obsession. I wanted to learn more about them.

Thanks to everyone who generously helped me document the lives of these pioneers. It is my sincere hope that I have captured the essence of truth in their lives.

PART I

The Land in the Beginning

My grandparents' homesteading story begins with the land.

The first men to walk this land—no doubt Native Americans—saw tall grasslands and the shallow, glacier-carved ponds and vast wetlands used by thousands of nesting birds.

A recent visit to a monument in the North Dakota of today reminds me that my grandparents were not the first people to consider the Northern Plains their home. More than a century after what was one of the biggest armed gatherings of Native American Indians on the continent, I examined a monument erected at Stony Lake Battleground. The marker is dedicated to the memory of the men of General Henry Hastings Sibley's expedition and the estimated 2500 Sioux warriors who battled them here in 1863. The message on the marker is tempered by time: "They all fought for what they thought was right."

This nearly forgotten battle, won decisively by the United States Army, helped end the Indians' nomadic life hunting buffalo (bison) on the land where my grandfathers later homesteaded. Although Indian tribes did not live year-round on that land, they regularly hunted buffalo there. They left trails and arrowheads behind, some of which my father later found on a high hill overlooking our farm. Dad particularly treasured several primitive stone hammers found in his field near depressions likely used as buffalo wallows. My brothers and I were allowed to admire the tools, but not to play with them.

The various Sioux tribes battled government forces again in various locales, notably Wounded Knee, before the final defeat of the Indians. Native Americans were subsequently sent to distant reservations, and the lumbering buffalo were nearly killed off. For a few decades the land stood largely empty except for fox, coyotes, prairie chickens, and countless waterfowl.

Although I grew up within twenty-five miles of the battlegrounds, I was oblivious to the earlier U.S. Army versus Indian battles that changed the course of history in the region. I never knew an Indian.

As a young child in 1953, I attended the dedication of a different monument in memory of Dr. Josiah S. Weiser, killed ninety years earlier at nearby Big Mound Battlefield. A neighbor explained to me that a savage had murdered the army doctor who was traveling with General Sibley. I learned that the low, grassy hills that stood a few miles south of our farm were named in Sibley's honor.

Later in school, I studied about the U.S. Army's Sibley Expedition that arrived in my homeland in 1863 to punish the Indians after the deadly Sioux Uprising in Minnesota a year earlier. I was too young to understand the bigger picture—a clash of two cultures over the same land.

Twelve years after Sibley's army detachment returned to Minnesota, the original U.S. government surveyors arrived in central North Dakota, in what is now northern Kidder County. They wrote in their journals that there was "not a tree in sight." They described the land my grandparents would homestead as rolling grassland, alkali lakes, ponds, and marshes with numerous Indian trails, but no rivers.

The Indian trails faded; the people who had used them were forgotten. The railroads arrived, bringing Norwegian and German settlers and a means to market their wheat crops. The pioneers turned the virgin sod with the plow; they dug wells, planted trees, built farms and roads, and divided up the land with barbed wire. The next generation installed power and telephone lines and paved highways.

My four grandparents arrived in North Dakota's Kidder County, beginning in 1905, from four different locales. They came by train to seize the opportunity of free land, opened to settlement by the expanding railroads.

Prairie pothole country itself remains as it has for generations. Family members were forever changed by their life on the prairie, yet the land and its uses stay constant.

This is my family's story.

Early scenes from Steele and Dawson in central North Dakota.

Prairie Justice

"All roads lead to Dawson, North Dakota," the city boosters declared in 1912. "This is a great place to live and raise children." The words had been true in this newly established community. Now the townspeople's sense of peace and security would soon be shattered.

Myrtle Baker's estranged husband, George, returned to Dawson on the eastbound No. 6 Northern Pacific train in the crisp, pre-dawn hours. The unlikely killer sat quietly in the depot waiting for daylight, and then headed to breakfast at the North Star Cafe. He heard the plaintive honking of the Canada geese flying south as he walked down Main Street carrying a shotgun and a small satchel.

Dawson citizens had regarded George Baker as a drifter and outsider. He had wooed young Myrtle in a brief courtship six years earlier while he worked on a threshing crew. They were married and left the area together. Gossips reported that Myrtle had become increasingly unhappy with Baker's itinerant lifestyle. After two children, Myrtle yearned to settle down. She eventually left him, bringing the children to Dawson to live with her recently widowed father, Thomas Glass. A few criticized Myrtle for running back home, but most felt sorry for her.

As Baker crossed the business section of town, he noticed several new shops and stores had sprung up since he'd last visited Dawson, but one hotel, the grand Sibley, named after the general, hadn't changed.

Spurred by glowing railway company propaganda, optimistic farmers and businessmen began pouring westward, bringing their families to the unspoiled Dakota prairie. For three decades the site of Dawson, North Dakota, had been the railroad terminus for homesteaders arriving in Kidder County. Now settlement was complete; the free land had been claimed.

European immigrants and settlers from states east and south of the Dakotas found a vast nothingness on which to build their new farming communities. They shared the land with waterfowl and small game—it was a hunters' paradise. In summer the pioneers encountered rich, rolling grasslands as far as they could see. In winter, frost and snow killed and flattened the tall grass, transforming the land into a white, unblemished canvas.

With the arrival of families and the building of churches and schools, life in Dawson had become downright civilized. The residents of this growing town prided themselves on their middle-class respectability.

A chill filled the air that November morning. The children of the Sibley Hotel proprietors, twelve-year-old Mary Eastburn and her seven-year-old sister, Abby, had just finished eating breakfast and were collecting their books and coats for school. Mary was moving slowly, not yet wide awake.

The girls eyed the serious, bespectacled telegraph operator who boarded in their hotel. He'd just finished his morning coffee.

"Look at Mr. Hanson. It must be Friday," Abby whispered. Mary nodded and giggled.

They'd made a game of telling what day of the week it was by judging how rumpled Mr. Hanson's suit, shirt, and tie looked. Each Monday Mr. Hanson appeared in clean, pressed clothes. He apparently slept in his clothes through the week without so much as loosening and re-tying his tie. By Friday his clothing appeared stained and disheveled.

"Mary, take this spool of white thread to Mrs. Baker before school, so she can finish the aprons," Mrs. Eastburn said. Mary nodded without comment.

Their seamstress, Mrs. Myrtle Baker, had been sewing white aprons for the hotel's kitchen staff. She lived nearby, but Mary wasn't in the mood to walk to Mrs. Baker's house in the crisp morning air. The aprons didn't interest her. Perhaps if the sewing involved a new dress, the task might've seemed more pressing. Mary dawdled, hoping to avoid the errand.

Meanwhile, across the street in the North Star Hotel, a group of men were eating breakfast when a stranger entered. Charles Smith, a local liveryman, noticed the short, ordinary-looking man. The visitor sat down and ordered a hearty breakfast of fried potatoes, ham, and eggs. When Smith got a coffee refill, he exchanged nods with the newcomer. Smith thought the man looked vaguely familiar, but didn't recognize him. He was probably a hunter. The customer complimented the staff and received seconds. After paying for his meal, he asked the cashier where Myrtle Baker lived.

"Lives with her father. Their house is the first one straight north down the road about five hundred yards. Can't miss it."

"Thanks," he said as he picked up his bag and gun and headed out. The stranger paused in the doorway, looked in the direction indicated, then disappeared down the rutted, unpaved side street.

Myrtle's neighbor lady, living in an adjoining apartment, heard a loud knock on the Glasses' front door. She later reported that Myrtle had exclaimed, "My God, Father, it's George."

The neighbor then overheard Glass assure Myrtle, "He can't hurt you," as the old man lumbered to the open door. Voices escalated in argument, then concluded with a loud command: "George, get the hell out of here."

A shotgun blast reverberated through the house.

The neighbor fled out the back door for help just moments before she heard a second shot.

Across town, a half hour after breakfast, Mrs. Eastburn spotted her daughter in the hotel lobby.

"Mary, haven't you left yet?" she asked. "I thought I told you to bring Mrs. Baker the thread before school."

Before Mary could answer, two liverymen rushed into the Sibley Hotel.

"They've been shot! Glass and his daughter," announced the one named Olaf.

Everything halted. School was forgotten. Everyone gathered to hear shocking news.

"What happened? Are they dead?"

"Yep, both of them," said Olaf.

"Oh my God, who did it?" asked Mrs. Eastburn.

"Her husband, George Baker."

"Where's he now?"

"Bon arrested him," Olaf said, referring to Dawson's town constable.

"The neighbors heard him quarrel with the old man. They heard two shotgun blasts," interjected the second liveryman. "Baker shot 'em dead. You hear shots?"

Several nodded. "Yeah. Didn't pay much attention. Thought someone was hunting."

When Constable Edgar Bon and three newly appointed deputies apprehended Baker, he was unarmed. Baker was carrying his young son, still in his nightclothes, away from the murder scene and toward the bar.

"Baker, where you going with the boy?"

"Don't want to leave him there without nobody to take care of him."

"How about giving us the little fellow. Don't want him to get hurt now, do you?" Bon asked. Baker complied, handing over the sobbing two-year-old to a deputy.

"You're under arrest," said the armed constable. Baker submitted without resistance.

"Where's the girl?" asked a deputy.

"Don't know."

The second deputy spoke up, "Mrs. Nelsen has her. She said the girl stayed overnight with her."

Both Myrtle and her father died on the spot in their home where they'd been having breakfast. Glass succumbed to a shot to the head. His daughter suffered a massive gunshot wound to the chest and bruises to her head, apparently from the butt of Baker's gun. The recently fired shotgun lay on the floor near the dead woman.

When Edgar Bon and the deputies subsequently returned with the suspect to the crime scene, Baker admitted he'd shot the victims, but he showed no remorse. He said little except that he killed the old man in self-defense. Baker sat on the bed at the murder scene, nervously rolling cigarettes until the Kidder County Sheriff arrived by horse and buggy. Sheriff Filiban transported the thirty-seven-year-old captive to the county jail in Steele, eight miles to the west, and booked him on charges of murder in the first degree. The news of the double murder spread like a prairie wildfire and shocked the little community where murder had been unknown.

The townspeople had respected Thomas E. Glass, age seventy, an early settler and Civil War veteran. Mr. Glass had been regarded as a good man, industrious and civic minded. "He wouldn't hurt nobody" became a common refrain in the days after the murders. The people of Dawson liked Glass's pretty daughter, Myrtle, and had patronized her home sewing business. Their funeral drew the largest crowd in memory. Emotions peaked and the townspeople murmured, "I wouldn't have recognized the poor thing. He must've beat her with his gun before he shot her."

Unsubstantiated rumors of Baker's prior harsh treatment and financial non-support of his wife grew wilder each day. One local newspaper reported, "It is said he was cruel to his wife." Baker waived examination, staying silent about the killings. He refused to give a statement to authorities. Baker displayed no remorse. This angered the "good citizens" of Dawson.

On November 7, one week after the funeral, the accused lay asleep behind bars upstairs in the county jail in Steele, his January trial still two months away. On midnight of that moonless night, noise awakened the janitor and the sheriff, sleeping in different parts of the large courthouse. The janitor stayed in bed, but the sleepy sheriff rose to investigate. County sheriff logs state that a mob of somewhere between fifteen and twenty-five men, their faces covered with handkerchiefs, burst into the second-floor corridor. They'd already sawed their way through five locks on the outer doors.

The mob overpowered the startled sheriff as he stepped into the narrow passageway leading to the jail cell without his gun.

"You're making a mistake. My God, go home," the sheriff pleaded in vain.

Remaining mute, several men physically restrained the sheriff, while others joined the ringleaders already cutting through the final lock to the jail cell that Baker shared with a man accused of larceny.

The terrified prisoners heard them coming. Baker begged for mercy. His fellow prisoner later reported he couldn't identify the voices in the mob, but he recalled the words a masked man had said to Baker: "You showed no mercy to your wife. We've come to get you."

They grabbed Baker and tied a thick rope around his neck.

A second man told the cowering fellow prisoner, "We're not after you. Mind your own business. Just keep looking out the window." He anxiously complied. True to their word, the men left him behind in the cell.

Baker, now choking, managed to squeak out one final desperate plea to the sheriff. Then silence. Still restrained and without a weapon, Sheriff Filiban was powerless to intervene.

The mob dragged Baker down the flight of stairs, out the front door, and down the street to the nearby stockyards. They hanged him from a wooden beam.

As soon as the remaining vigilantes freed him, Sheriff Filiban rushed to the phone in another part of the courthouse to call for help. Hastily putting on his coat and boots and lighting a kerosene lantern, he then followed drag marks in the snow. They led him to the prisoner, eyes bulging and limbs still twitching. Sheriff Filiban cut him down. Too late; he was already dead.

Eerie silence reigned on the dark street as the sheriff looked around. The mob had disappeared into the night as quietly as it had come, without leaving evidence.

The town buzzed with the news by dawn. Some citizens whispered the mob had used a special locomotive out of Jamestown for the trip from Dawson to Steele and back, but no one admitted to seeing or hearing anything, neither horses and wagons nor a train. After a few weeks and months, even speculation let up. Investigation into the identities of the vigilante mob reached a dead end. Silence became the byword for all participants in the well-planned lynching; no one was ever arrested for the crime, and all the nightriders apparently took the secret to their graves.

The official jail report (with original spelling errors) stated, "Linched by mob taking him out of jail and cutting thair way through 6 locks and put rope around is nick and draged him to the stock yards and hung to a beam."

Hearing all the talk, young Mary asked her father, "Pa, what's a lynching?" The terse response—"Don't know what you're talking about"—let Mary know never to speak of the incident in her home again.

Citizens did not blame the county sheriff; in fact, they re-elected him. The fact that the victims were an old man and a woman had enraged the townspeople. Editorial comments in the newspapers of the day varied; most declared it wrong to take the law into your own hands, but noted that, after all, Baker was guilty and got what he deserved—the violent murders justified the lynching. One friend of the Glass family remarked, "It wasn't exactly a lynching. They just dragged him with a rope until he was dead."

Such was "justice" in a small prairie town in 1912: prompt, deadly, and not subject to appeal.

Adria Williams, Paternal Grandmother.

Adria Williams, Paternal Grandmother: Petticoat Pioneer

My grandmother, Adria Williams, lived in the Sibley Hotel on weekdays when she arrived in North Dakota in 1908. The wooden three-story hotel on the prairie had been touted as one of the largest and finest in Dakota Territory when built in 1883 to herald the arrival of the railroad. The grand structure boasted over thirty rooms, not all heated.

Sibley Hotel, Dawson, ND

Adria stayed in a heated section of the hotel and ate her meals in the spacious dining room with two or three dozen long-term residents. She dined with railroad men, land office officials, and businessmen. College-educated and a former teacher of both children and adults, Adria worked as a stenographer during the busy homestead settlement period. Her boss was Mr. Posey, a one-armed lawyer and land agent—and bandit, as it turned out. Years later Mr. Posey was convicted of fraud and sentenced to the state prison. Adria expressed shock to discover her boss had been a con man.

On weekends during the growing season, Adria returned to her primitive homestead shanty. She was one of the "petticoat pioneers"—women who took land in their own name. "Good morning, Miss Williams. The coffee is especially good today. May I pour you a cup?" asked Mr. Johnson, a railroad agent, already seated at a long table covered with a crisp white tablecloth. Plentiful food, served family-style out of big white china bowls, sat on the table.

"Yes, sir. Thank you kindly," said Adria with a contagious smile. She situated herself and her bulky skirt and petticoats into an oak dining chair. "I detect a nip in the air this morning. Feels like autumn."

"Yes ma'am, indeed, it's harvest time. Your wheat harvested yet?" Mr. Johnson asked.

"No. Looks like a fine stand."

"Glad to hear it. Of course, you know nothing is certain in farming," Mr. Johnson said as he began his breakfast. "One hail storm can undo a whole year's work."

"Yes, but I'm hopeful."

Adria, a plump, thirty-year-old spinster, mixed easily with the men in the dining room, discussing the weather, farming, and the expectations for building a great city in Dawson. She took the advice of leading businessmen and invested in real estate lots in the newly plotted town.

At some meals Adria dined with liverymen who stabled and rented out horses. The liverymen discussed the impact of the new invention, automobiles. Other meals Adria shared with telegraph operators, real estate agents, bookkeepers, storeowners, and salesmen, as well as the local banker, the doctor, and a Congregational preacher who boarded at the hotel. At times Adria was the only woman guest, although wives and daughters resided there temporarily while their men built a home. The only other females, outside the proprietor's family, were the hotel cooks and chambermaids.

The Sibley's clean dining room featured wooden floors and kerosene lanterns hanging from the ceiling. Breakfast typically included eggs with ham or bacon, perhaps hot cereal, and always milk, buttered toast, and plenty of strong coffee. The noon and evening meals might feature roast chicken or beef, boiled potatoes and gravy, or perhaps beans and ham accompanied by biscuits. Seasonings and desserts varied with each cook.

Adria told of many visitors who stopped by this bustling railway hub. Occasionally, they would have a celebrity visitor, like James Hill, the railroad baron, or Thomas Slade, the state politician, who came to the area for its excellent waterfowl hunting.

Bathtubs and running water were not yet prairie amenities, but each hotel room contained a china pitcher, basin, and towel for personal bathing. Adria washed her wavy, brown hair with bar soap, as modern shampoo didn't exist. She was thankful she didn't have to pump the water, haul it inside, and heat it on the stove before washing up. And someone else disposed of the dirty bath water. What luxury! In addition, each room came equipped with a covered chamber pot for use during the night or on frigid below-zero mornings. Despite this being an upscale hotel, the toilet was a separate two-story wooden outhouse built adjacent to the hotel. The upper story was offset, so outhouse visitors were not situated directly over one another. While they could certainly hear other users, everyone pretended that they couldn't. The unpleasant odors were much harder to ignore, especially in the summer heat.

Adria and the other women didn't have to walk outside to visit the facilities. The women's downstairs section—a "two-holer" bench, accommodating both adult and child-sized bottoms—was accessible by the first-floor hotel exit. Men had to climb an additional outdoor flight of stairs or enter the second level of the outhouse from the second-floor hotel balcony to gain access to their "three-holer." The wastes collected in a large tray at the bottom that was pulled out by a team of horses and dumped some distance away at night.

The hotel staff sent the dirty sheets, towels, and kitchen linens to a laundry in Bismarck, fifty miles away by train. When it was time to wash or mend their clothing, hotel boarders hired local women to provide laundry service. This was one of the few means for prairie women to earn income.

One Monday morning Mary, twelve, and her mother were gathering the sheets in Adria's room when Mary moved one of Adria's long pleated skirts.

"Oh, my!" squealed Mary, dropping the heavy garment, when something—a grasshopper—jumped out onto her long brown cotton stockings. To her surprise, a dozen more grasshoppers darted out from among the pleats and hopped wildly around the small hotel room. Adria had spent the previous day at her country homestead; it seemed the pervasive hoppers hitched a ride to town in her billowing skirt.

"Catch them, Mary. We've got to get them all. Can't have grasshoppers inside," Mrs. Eastburn said crunching a long, skinny insect under her high-heeled boots. She bent down to scrape its mangled body off the wood floor and disposed of it. It was young Mary's task to squash or capture the remaining insects.

Williams family in 1891. From left, Bertis, father John Franklin Williams, Charles Spencer standing behind Edward, mother Mary holding Clarence, and Adria.

Mary Williams, Adria's mother.

Adria was born in Dakota Territory on January 18, 1882, a middle child and the only girl in a family of five boys, one of whom died in infancy. Her parents had homesteaded in 1880 near Fairmount, Richmond County, in eastern Dakota Territory. They arrived from Nebraska in a prairie schooner (covered wagon) pulled by a team of horses. Now a generation later, the Williams sons, Bertis and Edward, had grown to manhood. They moved westward from the Minnesota border to central North Dakota for land. Just as earlier generations had done, the young men followed the land available for homesteading. The opportunity brought them, via the railroad, to the new communities of Steele and Dawson.

Adria's parents had divorced after their children were grown. Her father, J. F. (John Franklin) Williams, stayed behind in Fairmount and later remarried. The law decreed single or widowed women were allowed to file for homesteads. Adria's mother, Mary Williams, was ineligible because she was a divorcée. Adria, unmarried, qualified to homestead. She and her two brothers filed homestead claims near each other.

The Williams family had prospered on their original wheat farm in the fertile Red River Valley. They emphasized education and rented a home in Wahpeton so the children could go to high school and college. Adria graduated from Wahpeton High School in 1899, and went on to a college education at Ellendale Normal School in eastern Dakota. She earned her degree in education, one of the few academic fields open to women, and then taught grades one through eight in one-room rural schools. An ambitious student herself, Adria next graduated from Aaker's Business College at Fargo, and later taught adult education there and in Milwaukee, Wisconsin. Upon arriving in Kidder County in 1908, she discovered they needed a stenographer for the land office. She knew shorthand and was immediately hired.

Although few women did so, Adria exercised the right to homestead on Section 12 in Manning Township in Kidder County, near her brothers' property. Adria's 160-acre homestead—one quarter of a square mile—stood on the same section as those belonging to Bertis (Bert) and Edward (Ed). The brothers' lands adjoined each other, so they built their barn on one side of the boundary and their house on the other side of it. Their mother, Mary, lived with them and kept house.

Mary Williams, described by relatives as a hearty, strong-willed woman, lived out the remaining forty years of her life in her new home in Steele. Mary never remarried. She died in 1946 at age ninety.

Adria's crude wood and tarpaper shack was built a half-mile away on her own land. Sparsely furnished, it provided a contrast to her comfortable hotel room. Adria managed her homestead, hiring her brothers to clear rocks from the land, to break the virgin soil to the plow, and to plant and harvest wheat. Those back-breaking tasks proved too physically demanding for most women.

All three siblings eventually met the legal requirements to "prove up" their claims, the commonly used term for fulfilling requirements, or proof, on federal land claims. All three became proud landowners. They believed land was the route to wealth.

The homestead laws varied from year to year. They generally required living on the land, at least during the growing season, from three to five years. Settlers had to make specified improvements, including planting at least twelve acres of the virgin grassland with grain. Each homesteader then made application for a homestead patent and paid certain fees. Each provided witnesses to vouch that he or she had resided on the property and met the additional requirements.

The land was nearly free, crop prices remained strong, and the future looked bright.

The Candidate

Adria moved to Steele and used her typing and steno skills in various county offices there, including working as Assistant County Superintendent of Schools. She grew tired of that job and decided to challenge her female boss in the 1916 elections—a risky decision.

"Good morning, ladies. What brings you to our fair city on such a warm summer day?" asked the editor, rising from his oak desk at the *Robinson Times*.

Adria Williams' candidate photo.

Adria removed her large sunbonnet, revealing a pleasant face and brown hair collected in an unruly bun. "Hello again, Mr. Flaherty. I'm Adria Williams, candidate for County Superintendent of Schools," she said extending her hand in greeting. "This is my driver, Miss Mary White."

Mary was the more slender of the two. Both young women appeared hot after their automobile ride in their high-collared, long-sleeved dresses, complete with bulky undercoats.

The gentleman in the newspaper office stepped forward and shook Adria's hand. "Yes, of course, Miss Williams, I recognize you. You visited us earlier. You made quite a strong showing in the primary here in Robinson. Some thought the incumbent would get most of the votes because she is from these parts. You did mighty fine. Pleased to meet you too, Miss White," he said shaking her hand. "What can I do for you today?"

"Well, I've been campaigning in the northern part of the county and thought I would stop by to place a thank-you note in the *Times*," Adria said.

"Certainly. Do you know what you wish to say?" Mr. Flaherty asked, reaching for a pad of paper.

"Oh, yes. I have the copy right here," Adria said, handing him a neatly typed sheet of paper.

"Let's see what you have here." He began reading aloud, "I wish to express my thanks to the voters of Kidder County, who so generously supported me in the recent primary election, thus assuring the appearance of my name upon the ballot for the November election. I again solicit your aid in a clean and winning campaign.   Adria H. Williams."

"Sounds fine to me," he responded, looking up over his spectacles. "We'll run it on Thursday. That'll be one dollar, please. Your chief opponent, Miss Hinman, called on us a couple days ago."

"Yes, she has spent considerable time here of late. But I'm confident I will make a good showing in November."

"Best of luck to you, Miss Williams. Let us know if we can do anything else for your campaign."

"Thank you. Be back in a week or two. I'll be running a political ad listing recommendations as soon as they are collected. I've received one so far. The others will be forthcoming. I've kept in touch with previous employers in the eastern part of the state before homesteading in Steele. They can attest to my teaching background."

"Excellent. I'll look forward to publishing that information."

"I hear your plans for building a new school are moving forward. A large consolidated school will be a wonderful addition to your growing community. Looks like prosperous country. We noticed four new barns being built on our way up here from Steele."

"Yes, the crops are better than ever. The Norwegian Lutheran church is nearly finished, and the Farmer's Union grain elevator will be complete before harvest. A modern brick school building with a full gymnasium is planned.

"Oh, Miss Williams," Flaherty continued, "I believe the Ladies Aid is meeting at the Madson farm just east of town this afternoon. You might have a chance to meet some of our fine womenfolk there. They can vote for you in the school election and influence their husbands' votes a great deal when it comes to schools. The women are the real driving force behind the plan to build the new school, you know. Have a fine day, ladies."

"Thank you for the suggestion. We may drive out that way to see the ladies. One of these years, hopefully soon, women will vote in all elections, not just certain contests."

Adria turned to leave. "We're driving to Hotel Robinson to eat just now. I hope to meet people and hand out more business cards during the noon meal." She nodded towards her companion, "Miss White has a real talent for handling these new automobiles."

"Oh, cars are fun to drive once you practice," Mary said giggling. "Good day, sir."

"Good day, ladies. Watch out for that puddle near the step. Good luck in your candidacy, Miss Williams. Come back any time."

Adria Williams was no stranger to politics. Although campaigning on a non-partisan ticket, she had grown up in a staunch Republican family. When I was growing up, we often heard the story of her mother, Mary, shaking hands with Abraham Lincoln at a political rally in Springfield, Illinois, back when Mary was a child.

Running second in the field during the primary election, Adria challenged her incumbent boss. Adria ran the following paid political advertisement in the *Robinson Times* in October of 1916, providing three references:

Grand Forks, N.D. May 24, 1916

To whom it may concern:

I have known Miss Adria H. Williams for the past thirteen years. She taught at Aaker's Business College in 1904 and her work was very satisfactory. She left my employ to accept a more lucrative position as a teacher in Milwaukee, and returned to Fargo to us in 1906, remaining until 1908 when she left for Kidder County, North Dakota.

I found Miss Williams a capable woman, thoroughly reliable, earnest in her work and exceedingly industrious.

Respectfully,
H. H. Aaker

Moorhead, Minn. Oct. 17, 1916

To whom it may concern:

This may certify that Miss Adria Williams is personally known to me, that she taught in the rural and graded schools of Richland County during my superintendency with splendid success. Miss Williams is a teacher of good character, earnest and progressive.

I recommend her as capable of large accomplishments wherever placed. She will do well whatever she undertakes.

O. J. Hagen, M.D.
County Superintendent,
Richland County
1898-1902

St. Paul, Minn. Oct. 12, 1916

Miss Adria Williams is not a relative, but a daughter of a friend living near Fairmount, N.D. Miss Williams is of a family much respected for their moral and social standing in a community where the parents were pioneers.

Miss Williams was a bright, progressive pupil and attained a good education. Her first teaching was in Traverse County, Minn. while I was county superintendent. Tho [*sic*] teaching a difficult school, she was highly successful and possessed those qualities of mind and heart that insure successes in life.

It is a pleasure to give to one so deserving a testimonial to her work and worth.

W. T. Williams

Supervising Schoolmarms

Would Adria's personal reputation, numerous personal appearances, and political advertising be enough to win the election? Yes: She won handily in November, 1916, and took on her new duties the next January. I wish I had been there to congratulate her. Her boss went back to teaching, so in an ironic twist, Adria now supervised her former boss.

At the time of her election, North Dakota women still weren't allowed to vote except in school matters. I am proud that my paternal grandmother was an early leader in women's rights. A former teacher, she was responsible for overseeing ninety-seven North Dakota schools, all but seven of which were one-room rural schools in 1917. Her teaching staff consisted of ninety-nine female teachers and eighteen male teachers.

Adria Williams as Kidder County Superintendent of Schools.

◆   ◆   ◆

Male teachers earned an average of nearly sixty dollars per month for a seven- or eight-month term. Females earned eighty-nine percent of what their male counterparts received. Adria advocated boosting the prevailing wage to attract better-qualified teachers, both men and women.

With a salary of $125 a month, Adria was no doubt the highest paid woman in the county. The short, plump spinster with a contagious smile shouldered considerable responsibility. Her duties included overseeing teacher recruitment, training, examination, and certification. Upgrading teacher qualifications became her primary goal. As the county's chief educator, Adria believed passionately that, "the major component of a good school is a dedicated, qualified instructor."

A typical rural classroom on the North Dakota prairie housed anywhere from ten to thirty children spread over eight grades, with a sole teacher. Instructors signed individual contracts with the local farmers who served as directors for their neighborhood school. These men often had little formal education themselves. They often judged teachers as much on their housekeeping abilities and their Christmas and patriotic programs as on their disciplinary or teaching skills.

The considerable physical demands on a rural teacher in pioneer times were daunting. The teacher's contract usually stipulated many demanding janitorial duties, such as hauling water, cleaning the outhouses, and keeping the coal stove functioning in the drafty wooden classroom. The schoolmarm had to arrive well before the students to carry in the day's supply of coal from the nearby coal shed and start the fire in the pot-bellied stove. She couldn't go home in the evening until she'd banked the fire into a tight heap so the embers would slowly burn out. Then she could safely leave the coal stove unattended. Few early schools had wells, so she hauled drinking water from the nearest farm. If she were lucky, older boys helped carry things.

Moreover, each instructor was entrusted with the health and safety of the neighborhood children. Isolated rural schools, vulnerable to prairie fires and blizzard, had no phones. The pioneers knew that natural forces had claimed school children's lives. The tragic story of six North Dakota students and their schoolmarm, victims of a prairie fire in 1914, remained fresh in the public's awareness.

Besides rigorous janitorial and teaching duties, each instructor was accountable for the onerous task of maintaining a written register detailing all school activities. To discourage a teacher from walking away from the reporting, the last month's salary could be withheld until all reports were filed and approved by the County Superintendent of Schools.

Historically, educational objectives before 1900 centered on turning out good human beings, not necessarily clever ones. Early Course of Study materials stated that "All good teaching has a potent moral element." They continued, "The one vital condition of effective moral instruction is character in the teacher," elaborating in great detail. In fact, the following examples from that era give pause to anyone who advocates equal rights for women. One of the earliest instructions to teachers for Dakota Territory in 1872 states: "Women teachers who marry or engage in other unseemly conduct will be dismissed." However, men teachers could "take one evening each week for courting purposes or two evenings a week if they go to church regularly." The same instructions warned that "any teacher who smokes, uses liquor in any form, frequents a pool or public hall, or gets shaved in a barber shop will give good reason for suspecting his worth, intentions, integrity and honesty."

Moral expectations in the profession ran high. The instructor was expected to practice—as well as teach—good hygiene, industriousness, patriotism, prohibition, and disciplined moral behavior, besides covering an academic course of study. Teachers opened the day with the pledge to the flag and a Bible reading. Essentially, instructors served as moral role models.

The community held their teachers in high esteem, but at a price. Schoolmarms were socially restricted, almost like nuns. Instructors endured constant surveillance from the local citizens. Their lifestyle and associations were widely discussed: Some had to accept employment contracts that imposed nightly curfews; most instructors were expected to attend whatever church was available and volunteer in the community. The local directors, all men, had the power to fire their teacher for "immoral" actions, however they might judge such activities. Such decisions could be appealed to the County Superintendent of Schools, but rarely were contested. Once a teacher's reputation became tarnished, she had little choice but to move.

Because men dramatically outnumbered woman on the prairie, keeping young women, average age twenty-two, in the teaching pool was problematic. Schoolmarms moving into a new community encountered many eligible suitors. Each year scores of young women left the teaching profession to marry and rarely taught after marriage. School directors were pragmatic about keeping the classroom open, adhering to the idea of "No teacher, no school. Gotta make sure they don't get in a family way or get married." In order to discourage turnover, local contracts often contained anti-marriage clauses for women. If a woman teacher married, she voided her contract and often forfeited part of her meager salary. If she became pregnant, the school board dismissed the teacher, even if her vacancy closed the school. After all, they couldn't have an obviously pregnant teacher in the classroom.

As overseer of the moral instructors of the county's youth, Adria was mandated to visit each school and "carefully observe the condition of the school, the mental and moral instruction given, the methods of teaching employed by the teacher, the teacher's ability, and the progress of the pupils." She prepared a written evaluation of each instructor's ability for the local directors. If teachers didn't succeed, it reflected poorly on the superintendent and her office.

Public scrutiny of my grandmother as County Superintendent of Schools was intense in a man's world. No one formally defined what place in the community that public official held, but it was common knowledge she should "keep her place." She faced election every two years by the mostly male electorate. Few women voted, as they were limited to a few school elections and dependent on their men to take them to the polls.

◆   ◆   ◆

The subject of hiring standards for teachers came up at an annual meeting of local school board directors. "The teacher shortage in Dakota isn't that great," Adria told the gathering. The thirty-five-year-old educator patted back her brown, wavy hair straying from her bun. "We'll have enough certified applicants without hiring those lacking permits. Those who failed the recent exam need additional training before they are retested."

Although the directors listened respectfully, this day Adria lost the argument. "Miss Pederson will make a fine teacher," they assured her. "We know she comes from an upstanding family. Never know what a stranger might teach our children. Someone has to board an outsider while Miss Pederson could remain at home."

If the teacher didn't already live in the area, the directors had to locate a family who could board the instructor for a fee, ideally within a two-mile walk of the schoolhouse. The schoolmarm was responsible for paying her board and room.

The local applicant, Miss Pederson, was a recent high school graduate who'd completed a college summer course, but hadn't yet acquired teacher certification. Adria realized that the uncertified teacher would work at a lower pay rate, and finances often topped other considerations. Although state aid helped, most of an instructor's salary came from taxes levied on local farmers.

The board knew this young teaching candidate's lifestyle, but Adria wondered if she had acquired the needed teaching skills. Adria understood their desire to hire within the community. Sometimes it worked well. Her own aunt, Jenny Williams, had taught Adria in a one-room school. Adria herself taught in country schools near her home after she finished teacher training. Plus, when it came to finances, Adria had better luck soliciting money for practical matters—such as repairing the schoolhouse roof, plowing up the sod for firebreaks around the schoolyard, or maintaining a bigger coal supply for the classroom stove—than for paying a teacher enough to cover room and board.

Educational expectations hadn't changed much by 1917, when Adria led the county's program. However, one recent law proved difficult to enforce, especially with some of the newest immigrants: North Dakota began mandating compulsory attendance for children eight to fourteen years old. Adria passionately supported the attendance rule. In her annual report to the State Superintendent of Schools, she wrote, "One of my goals is to standardize the subjects taught in a goodly number of the rural schools. I believe that a good school is the best persuader to the parent and pupil. Good schools will encourage better attendance. "

One afternoon Adria expressed frustration regarding school truancy. She was visiting with the state's attorney in the new courthouse where they both worked. "I must coax more children into school," she told him. "I've tried starting the term later when the harvest is complete. I'll make another appeal at the upcoming social meetings."

"Did delaying the school term help?" the attorney asked.

"Yes, but there's a problem in the immigrant community south of town. They don't yet see the value of schooling their older children. Some of the German-Russians don't understand the truancy laws, or simply ignore them. They need the children to work more hours on the farm. Most of their children don't know English, so it's a difficult situation."

Adria was referring to a group of German-born farmers who had first relocated to Russia, then left its grassy plains for North Dakota. They considered themselves German-Americans, not Russian-Americans. They had retained their language and cultural traditions in Russia and continued to do so in America.

Adria continued, "We really need German-speaking teachers. We don't have any at present. It's hard to match a family with a teacher boarder when the family doesn't speak English."

"Miss Williams, I agree we must improve our attendance. It affects our state aid," the attorney said.

"Yes," said Adria, "Now North Dakota requires a system for reporting non-attendance, similar to the county one we devised earlier. It's flattering to know we used one first."

The attorney smiled and nodded in agreement.

Adria went on, "We'll use the state's new forms in addition to our current parents' affidavits explaining why their children are not attending and when they expect to send them to school. We must pressure the parents."

The attorney shifted in his big leather chair, "Yes, we need better enforcement of the existing laws. Not much help from the attorney general."

"You're absolutely right," Adria concurred. "He's afraid he'll lose immigrant votes if he enforces the truancy laws." She rose to leave. "Well, must get back to my formal reports. I provide statistics on everything from my school inspections to schoolyard trees planted. I've considerable work to complete before the filing deadline."

A Life-changing Moment
Under the Big Top

Ed Williams, Adria's brother.

Edward Williams, Adria's brother, knew life was not fair, but believed he was lucky, at least most of the time. My great-uncle Ed, born in Dakota Territory ninety years earlier, relished retelling the story of what happened in June, 1897, when he was a boy of twelve. My brothers and I loved to hear the tale.

The much-anticipated day had finally arrived: The famous Ringling Brothers Circus traveled via railroad to Ed's hometown of Wahpeton in the newly formed state of North Dakota. Ed had no money for the circus performance, so he was anxious to earn a ticket to the show. Heavy rain didn't dampen his spirits when he eagerly woke before dawn. He dressed quickly and even skipped breakfast, hoping to be the first in line to secure a job helping the circus crews set up. Indeed, Ed was one of the lucky few chosen by the circus foreman.

Using a block and tackle, the young boys struggled under the canvas to raise the massive tent, designed for 10,000 people. Torrential rains during the night had filled the deep folds of the canvas with tons of water, making it too heavy to lift.

The foreman slashed the canvas to lighten it, freeing a deluge of water onto the ground around them. Despite their best efforts, the boys couldn't budge the heavy canvas. Tired and cold, the boys had wet feet and aching arms. Their hands grew raw from tugging on the drenched ropes. Gusting winds, heavy rain, and soggy ground had made their task nearly impossible. Finally a group of veteran circus roustabouts impatiently moved in to complete the job.

"I was pulling on the rope when one big fellow pushed me aside saying, 'This is a man's work!'" Ed remembered.

Just as Ed let go of the rope and stepped back, he saw a blinding flash. A deafening clap of thunder enveloped them. A bolt of lightning had struck the towering center pole.

The burly crewmember who'd taken Ed's place seconds before lay dead, electrocuted. A second worker died beside him. Several other workers were knocked unconscious onto the wet ground. Crew men frantically resuscitated the injured men by beating on the bottoms of their feet and rubbing their palms. They revived, although one of them died a year later of his injuries.

Miraculously, Ed and the local boys walked away shaken, but unhurt. Ed realized he had cheated an early death. He felt blessed, lucky to have a future.

Circus personnel quickly notified the families of the victims by telegraph. They followed the families' wishes to bury the men in a nearby Bohemian Cemetery that afternoon.

The circus personnel collected an astounding $500 from among their own to design and sculpt a granite grave marker. The six-foot-tall monument depicts the tent with a shattered center pole and deep crack left by the lightning bolt. The center pole is carved with a chain and rope used to raise the canvas.

Two Views of Circus Monument, Wahpeton, ND.

Ed's story came to life for me when I visited the monument over one hundred years later. I could still read the inscription on the front of the tent-shaped base: "Erected by the employees of the Ringling Brothers Circus," along with a carving of the symbols of canvas men, a tent stake and hammer. The names and dates of the victims—Charles Smith and Chas. E. Walters—were chiseled on the sides of the granite base.

The unique monument has been described as the most significant memorial in the circus world. The sculptor is unknown, but the tall marker standing above the flat prairie landscape remains impressive, evoking memories of the traveling circus.

On the day of the accident the bosses eventually decided, "The show must go on." Circus personnel belatedly began the magnificent parade from the railroad siding in Wahpeton across the Red River Bridge to the circus grounds in Breckenridge, Minnesota. About 650 colorfully costumed circus members marched with the circus animals. Painted wagons and a whistling steam calliope slowly wound through the muddy streets.

Ed told us he had been captivated with the largest animals. He watched the dazzling show horses, elephants, and the biggest hippopotamus imaginable. The heavy wagon carrying the hippo became mired in mud. Eight horses failed to pull it free. A shove by a huge elephant finally nudged it loose.

Ed tried to collect the circus ticket he'd earned. It was only fair. Not content to just watch the grand parade, he caught the attention of a costumed horseman. Ed yelled up to him explaining that although he'd worked on the tent, he hadn't received his circus ticket.

The horseman inquired, "Where's your foreman?"

"He's dead," Ed shouted.

"Hard luck!" the performer replied, and rode away.

Thomas Arthur Price, Paternal Grandfather.

Thomas Arthur Price, Paternal Grandfather: Sodbuster and Keeper of the Peace

"You can't survive a North Dakota winter without heat," Dad used to say. That point was vividly illustrated when he told us tales of his father, Thomas Price. As we listened one February night, my brother and I cuddled in a little closer as we heard the howling wind rattle our farmhouse windows. We shuddered to think of spending even one night minus the warmth of our pot-bellied stove.

Tom Price homesteaded in south-central North Dakota, arriving in the fall of 1905. He settled the newly available land near the railroads as their secondary branches pushed westward through the Dakotas and Montana. Settlement followed the rails, and over 500 miles of railroads were constructed in North Dakota in 1905. Unlike a typical family man who'd left his father's farm in Minnesota or Iowa to go west, Tom arrived from South Dakota alone. He was a thirty-seven-year-old bachelor.

Everyone who remembered Tom described him the same way. He stood tall, an imposing man with broad shoulders and a military bearing. He prided himself on his long, black mustache, waxed into a handlebar shape.

As Tom groomed his thick mustache one morning, he remembered his brother, Will, and their friendly rivalry over which one grew the best mustache. They sent each other photo postcards exhibiting their best growth. Not bad, Tom thought as he waxed it. The mirror revealed his dark eyebrows, vivid blue eyes, and long nose. If only he had hair. A bout of typhoid fever caused him to bald early. Tom donned his favorite black derby, concealing his nearly bald head. He grinned as he thought of a conversation with a child who had asked, "Why don't you have any hair?"

"I gave it to the dolls so they can have hair," he'd told her.

Like other arrivals, Tom had been enticed by free land. He'd already tried numerous ventures, including sodbusting for hire throughout the Northern Plains and cattle wrangling in Idaho. He'd farmed grain with his father, Daniel, in South Dakota, and raised cattle and horses on his own.

Tom abandoned his ranching plans when eighty head of his cattle and several horses were lost in a barn fire. Tom had loved his huge Percheron draft horses: even years later, tears welled up in his eyes when he thought of the animals lost in the tragedy. Only the team he was using at the time of the fire was spared. That horrible fire cast a long shadow over Tom's future business decisions. Later, when forced to make a choice, he chose to pay fire insurance over property taxes.

Devastated by his loss, Tom had packed up and started over, heading to central North Dakota and filing a homestead claim on Section 14-142-72 in Kidder County. An early pioneer, he was one of a handful to spend the winter of 1905-06 in this desolate, largely uninhabited region.

Tom's homestead shanty.

My grandfather underestimated how frigid his lumber and tarpaper shack would become during minus-forty-degree weather with gale-force winds. He credited the body heat of his tan bulldog companion for getting him through the first winter storm. "I would've frozen to death if it hadn't been for old Rex," Tom told the Dawson storekeeper. "My dog curled up next to me to help keep me warm, or I might not have made it."

Tom had made the full-day trip to Dawson by horse and sled to stockpile more coal for his potbelly stove. "Ran out of coal. Didn't expect a three-day blizzard so early. Learned a hard lesson. Only thing left to burn was my wooden table and chairs."

As his team made its way back to his homestead shanty, Tom was visually reminded that the treeless prairie provided no natural trees for fuel, unlike his native Michigan. The buffalo chips burned by the first white men in Dakota had long since been depleted. No fences existed yet; no trees had been planted on the new homesteads. Settlers hadn't accumulated straw piles or corncobs they could use for fuel. The long, prairie grass, a fire hazard in summer, remained buried under deep snowdrifts.

A student of history, Tom knew the Sioux Indians had left a generation earlier, and the last buffalo herds had been wastefully slaughtered by white hunters. Now a handful of settlers' homes dotted the rolling, tall-grass prairie, devoid of trees. The sparse population contributed to the feeling of loneliness, and for Tom, the monotony of that first winter seemed endless. As an isolated homesteader before the advent of radio, he had nothing but his dog to keep him company. Nightfall brought utter darkness; he could travel for miles in any direction without seeing the light of a single kerosene lantern. But he knew the wild animals watched his every move. The bone-chilling cry of coyotes punctuated the howling wind.

In the spring of 1906, dozens of farmers and would-be farmers arrived in Dawson by train. They loaded their wives and children and their belongings into teams and wagons for the final fifteen to twenty miles of their journey.

Tom wholeheartedly welcomed neighbors. They filed claims on the newly available land promoted by the railroads. The settlers not only established a fresh life for their families, but also formed a community, the town of Robinson. Tom noticed many neighbors and extended families, often siblings and cousins, arrived after having traveled together from eastern states. Others were European immigrants who had just arrived in America. Tom found he had trouble communicating with them in English. Most settlers were poor, with a few exceptions; the wealthy ones recognized the opportunity of free land and a booming economy and had the capital to expand.

Some of Tom's new neighbors stayed with him in his shanty while they built their own shacks. "Thanks for your hospitality," they said. "We won't forget your kindness."

Tom lived on the property for the five years required to "prove up" or qualify for ownership. Tom celebrated when he was granted the deed (patent) from the United States government giving him title to 160 acres of his own land with a signature seal from President Chester A. Arthur. At long last a landowner, Tom savored the moment of success.

Early views of Robinson, ND, circa 1915. Tom drives one of the town's early automobiles near his livery stable. Photos by Carl Wick.

◆   ◆   ◆

In 1911, the village of Robinson, named for an area banker, sprang up three miles to the north of Tom's homestead, along a new branch line of the Northern Pacific Railroad. The government gave the railroad companies considerable acreage along their railway lines. They established little towns every ten miles, about a day's drive by horse and wagon. The railroads often sold the remaining land to investors and speculators.

Robinson soon boasted a post office, general merchandise store, and a newspaper. They finished the store building in time to hold a Fourth of July dance before stocking it with merchandise to supply the homesteaders. Tom no longer had to travel to Dawson for supplies, some twenty miles to the south by prairie trail.

Crops were good. A building boom followed. Within a few months, the Konningrud Brothers Blacksmith Shop, Winner Adams Lumber Yard, Robinson Hotel, City Pool Hall, plus a meat market and barber shop were established there. Three grain elevators were constructed to hold the anticipated wheat and barley harvests. In 1912, Tom built a livery stable in the bustling town so he could board horses for visitors. He maintained teams, wagons, and drivers for rent—and he also embraced technology.

In spite of working with horses all his life, he was intrigued by the new invention, the automobile. I can imagine his neighbors' surprise when Tom arrived in an auto.

"Have you seen Tom's vehicle?" asked Nils, a neighbor. "He drove a 1911 Model T Ford into Robinson yesterday. Tom told me he bought it from Dr. Pryse in Dawson."

"No, haven't seen it yet. Heard plenty about it," said another neighbor.

"It's quite a contraption, shiny black, but noisy. Guess he's going to use the auto in his livery. Do you think they'll catch on?"

"No. Just a passing fancy. Don't know why everyone is so excited. I wouldn't pay to ride in that thing. Horses are safer and a lot more reliable."

Of course, the automobile didn't go away. Tom kept the auto and enjoyed the attention wherever he drove it, although it was useless in snow.

◆   ◆   ◆

Tom's first farm house.

After a couple years, Tom resumed full-time farming. He exchanged the livery stable for the homestead of William and Dora Moores, operators of the Robinson Hotel. That enlarged their operation and gave Tom the security of owning more farmland. My grandfather always trusted the land, looking on it at the primary source of wealth.

"Tom, why don't you run for sheriff?" urged his neighbors. Tom filed for Kidder County Sheriff in 1915, and easily won. Tom and his neighbors saw a future full of promise in the open prairie. He believed that with sacrifices he could tame the land, and it would fulfill his dreams. The pioneers passed that vision (or was it stubborn commitment?) on to their children, notably my father, Bruce. Indeed, the plains became the breadbasket of America within one generation of its settlement.

But Tom's personal dreams of prosperity never materialized.

Feud Turns to Murder

The murder committed during Sheriff Tom Price's watch happened near Robinson, North Dakota, in December, 1916.

My paternal grandfather, Tom, had saved newspaper columns describing the murder and the suspect's capture, keeping them in his black satchel—the one Dad kept tucked away for decades after Tom's death. I had heard the stories Dad told about Grandpa Tom, but now I relished reading the yellowed clippings. I noted discrepancies among the newspaper accounts themselves, but saw a clear picture unfold of "Tom, the County Sheriff."

Dad told us with obvious pride that people had trusted Tom. Old-timers who remembered my grandfather recounted how he had enjoyed a good reputation. His contemporaries regarded my grandfather as levelheaded and honest, willing to take a stand in tough situations. In a community where a handshake sealed business deals, reputation mattered. We reaped the benefit of growing up with Tom's surname.

The county's first settlers were primarily single men, followed by families. Although generally law-abiding, the pioneers were a self-reliant group, averse to government interference. One hot-button issue caused controversy among them: alcohol.

State prohibition laws had been adopted by a slim margin, and North Dakota entered the union as a dry state in 1889. Citizens, especially newspaper editors, held strong opinions, pro and con. Bootlegging was a crime punishable by penitentiary imprisonment. Men remained divided about whether the state's prohibition laws should be vigorously enforced. Many of the women, who couldn't vote yet, appeared inclined to oppose alcohol. Although not everyone embraced temperance, state law mandated teaching abstinence from alcohol to schoolchildren. County sheriff's arrest records show Tom arrested men for such crimes as larceny, jumping their bill at the local hotel, assault, and wife desertion, but mostly bootlegging.

Always pragmatic, Tom tried to contain the well-established bootlegging industry. An aunt later told me Tom once paid a business call on my maternal grandfather, Gust, to investigate rumored alcohol violations. Grandfather Gust was questioned but never arrested. When called upon to arrest former neighbors for liquor law violations, Tom maintained, "I'm sworn to uphold the law, even if I don't always agree with it."

One October day, Cleon "Smokey" Nash and Clarence Hicks, farmers living in northern Kidder County, had ended up in a drunken brawl. No one knew the root cause, but locals blamed bootleg whiskey for the tragic outcome. Hicks emerged with a badly cut-up face. Their festering animosity far outlasted their hangovers.

Two months later on a bitter cold Sunday afternoon, twenty-nine-year-old Nash, his anger stoked with booze, stomped across the frozen prairie to his neighbor's farm home. Again, no one knew what provoked this particular trip. It wasn't a friendly visit. Carrying his rifle, he angrily marched up to Hicks' front door and banged on it. When a boy working for Hicks answered the door, Nash pointed the gun at the lad and yelled, "Get the hell out of here, or I'll shoot you."

The boy grabbed his coat and high-tailed it for the next farm. He didn't dare look back, although he heard shouting and the crack of gunfire. Nash slunk back home and told his horrified wife, "I shot Hicks. Could be dead. Always said he'd shoot me, but I got it done first. Send a kid over to find out if I killed him."

Nash left in haste, making his December getaway on foot, because the pioneer family didn't own a horse or a car. He headed north across the snow-covered countryside. Mrs. Nash bundled up against the cold and walked to the neighbor's place to investigate, terrified of what she might find. She trudged up about the same time two farmers happened to drive by in a car. She hailed them, and while sobbing, told them the story. The men cautiously entered Hicks' homesteading cabin with their weapons drawn while she paced nervously outside.

They discovered a grim scene. Clarence Hicks lay dead on the floor in a pool of blood, shot point blank. The bullet had ripped through the chest, just below the heart.

After calming the distraught woman, the men drove into Robinson to report the murder to Deputy Brown. He collected the body, then deputized the two farmers, asking them to remain overnight at the crime scene. "Take your guns and remain on guard in case Nash comes back," he said. But Nash never showed up.

Deputy Brown reported the crime to his superior, my grandfather, at the courthouse in Steele, a half-day journey by horse to the south. Everyone expected Nash to flee north to the train in the next town, Carrington. The following morning Deputy Brown and a local citizen, Doc Baird, tracked the suspect north from his home for five miles before the trail "went cold" because fresh snow covered the footprints. The new snowdrifts made the roads impassable for cars, so the settlers were relegated to horses for the duration of the long winter.

The searchers returned empty-handed. Authorities sent telephone and telegraph messages alerting towns around the state to arrest Nash on sight, describing him as short, with blue eyes and brown hair. They also tried to locate the victim's relatives in Kentucky. All the while, gossips condemned law authorities for allowing the whiskey-fed, long-running feud between two neighbors to get out of hand, yet no one had offered a solution to end the dispute.

Meanwhile, the bitter cold spell complicated Nash's escape. When he didn't show up at the Carrington train station within three days, most people figured he'd frozen to death or turned the gun on himself. Other neighbors nervously speculated about Nash's return. "I sure don't want to meet up with him," was heard in the streets. "He might do something crazy."

"Yeah, what's to stop him from killing again?"

Nash remained alive and on the lam, hiding by day and traveling by night. He later admitted he hadn't been able to locate the railway station, becoming hopelessly lost on the endless expanse of white prairie. In fact, Nash had attempted to return to the crime scene, but became disoriented and drifted three miles off course. Then he spotted a vacant shack. The abandoned wooden shelter had no food or heat, but it provided more protection than the piles of straw where he'd been hiding. All the while, a nervous community kept reporting possible sightings.

Nine days after the killing, a traveler stopped to water his horses at the abandoned building where Nash hid. The passerby saw something move inside the shack and walked closer to investigate. The fugitive, still armed, opened a window and yelled, "For God's sake, call Sheriff Price at Steele. I shot a man. I'm freezing to death. I'll give myself up to Price, but no one else."

The wayfarer confirmed Nash's fear that Hicks had died, then rode on, reporting the incident to the Robinson deputy who phoned the county sheriff. Tom responded, "Can't get away today. Got some pressing court deadlines. I'll come in the morning."

Tom dreaded the frigid thirty-mile trip, but left by horse before first light. En route, he picked up a sled and deputized a trusted neighbor, John

Wilkins, to accompany him on the arrest. The temperature had dropped to thirty degrees below zero. Looking like a giant bundled against the frigid temperatures, Tom approached the cabin and called to Nash.

"Glad to see you, Price. Can't stand the cold," Nash said. True to his word, the suspect handed over his gun and surrendered without incident. "Yeah, I shot him, but he threatened me first."

Finding Nash in bad shape, Tom took him directly to the hospital in Steele. He had frozen his nose, face, feet, and hands. Doc Evans saved his fingers, but gangrene had set in on his feet. The jailer later told Tom that he was surprised Nash didn't freeze to death.

"Yeah, sure could have, even on the way back. What a miserable, godforsaken trip!"

"I'll bet."

"Took me all day by horse and sled. Nearly killed my horse. Worried about getting frostbite myself. Was chilled to the bone," Tom said. "Doc Evans did the best he could. Saved his fingers. They had to amputate part of both feet in Bismarck."

That week the editor of the *Robinson Times*, obviously not a fan of the Republican Sheriff, wrote a scathing editorial. He declared the state's attorney and county sheriff hadn't enforced the liquor laws, in effect contributing to the crime. The editor wrote, "Our brave (?) Sheriff was 'too busy' to try to capture Nash. Things have come to a pretty pass, indeed, when the decent, law-abiding citizens of this community can get no protection from the officers of the law against this gun-toting, gambling and bootlegging element which, unfortunately, we have in our midst …"

The editor continued, asserting, "No wonder that Robinson has the name of being one of the toughest towns in the northwest." The newsman offered a suggestion. "It is high time that this section of Kidder County was cleaned up, and if the gentlemen elected by the taxpayers to enforce the law are afraid to perform their duty, we would advise the decent and fearless citizens to turn themselves into a vigilante committee, take the law in their own hands."

Tom dismissed the editorial as political hyperbole and began preparing for the county's first murder trial. (The last murder suspect never made it to trial.)

Concern for his security may have prompted Nash to surrender only to the county sheriff and be jailed in the county seat, not his hometown. He trusted Tom to get him to safety. Nash no doubt understood he was lucky to secure a trial, not a lynching, as was the case for the only other murderer in the county's short history. Remembering the fate of that incarcerated man, the killer probably worried that his neighbors might break him out of jail and hang him before his trial could begin.

Tom openly admitted the Robinson jail wasn't secure. He described it in practical terms: "It's mostly used to dry out drunks. When they sober up, they simply break jail."

Everyone knew it wouldn't slow down a hanging party.

Months later, Nash appeared at his trial crawling on his hands and knees, but that sight didn't elicit much sympathy. Convicted of murder, he was sentenced to a life term in the North Dakota State Penitentiary. This time, justice played out in the courtroom instead of on the streets, although the threat of vigilante justice and eye-for-an-eye mentality lingered.

My grandfather had summed up those times when moral codes were more rigid this way: "A killer is probably safer in jail than running around loose in these parts."

Sheriff Price Returns Home
for Christmas

"You're home. Right on time," said Polleet (Polly), age eighty, her eyes lighting up as she spotted her second-oldest son, Thomas. She straightened her striped apron and patted back her gray hair. Thomas strode across her kitchen. Reece, who had met his brother at the train depot in Aberdeen, South Dakota, followed. Tom set down his black satchel and greeted his mother. It was December 24, 1916.

"Thomas. Now let me get a good look at you," she said adjusting her spectacles and stretching out her aging hands to her tall son. "Why, I believe you've put on a couple pounds since last summer. Must be eating well."

"Yes. Always do better on someone else's cooking. Cafeteria meals."

"I've cooked up your favorite beef roast tonight for your birthday. Hard to believe you turned forty seven today." Polly smiled at her son. "It seems like only yesterday you were born back in Michigan. Tom, our Christmas Eve baby."

Moments later Daniel Price, the eighty-year-old patriarch, entered the tidy kitchen. Daniel carried himself with authority in spite of a slight stoop and an old logging injury that had partially disabled one arm. His injury dated back to his youthful days as an Indian trader on Lake Huron. "Good to have you home, son. How's the train ride?"

"No problem. Ran on time. Surprised you don't have snow. We already had several inches when I boarded back in Steele."

"Been mild so far. Lots of time for snow," said Daniel.

Tom sniffed the mingling aromas of freshly baked bread, roast beef, apples, and cinnamon. "Smells good in here, Ma," Tom said, turning to his mother at the cook stove.

Polly and Daniel Price, Great-grandparents. He wears Grand Army of
the Republic medals. Elderly Daniel.

Polly nodded, smiling, then gestured them toward the living room.
"Move along so we can get the food on the table."

The men entered the adjoining room. Daniel eased into his favorite
oak rocking chair, the one in which he rocked his grandchildren when they
visited. Tom remembered his father holding grandchildren on his knee
and serenading them with his favorite Civil War song, "Marching through
Georgia."

Tom looked forward to seeing his sister, Kit, and his brother, George,
recently married. He inquired about the seven siblings scattered around the
country. "Heard from the rest of the family?"

"Yes, got Christmas letters from everyone. They're all doing fine."

Daniel continued, "So tell me, Thomas, how's the job of county sheriff?
You haven't had any more of those lynchings like the Baker affair a couple
years back, have you?"

"No, Pa, it's been quiet until recently. Had my first murder." Tom then
relayed the Nash murder story to rapt attention.

"Enforcing the state's prohibition laws is what keeps me busy. Had to
confiscate a rather large supply recently in Pettibone, east of Robinson.
Seemed such a shame to destroy good whiskey, but I've sworn to uphold the
law, such as it is."

"Seems to be plenty of spirits around, considering North Dakota is a dry state," added Tom's brother, Reece.

Tom continued. "Most of my arrests have been for stealing and bootlegging, or someone overdoing booze. Had a burglary in the railroad depot at Dawson. The lad was caught red-handed with the sixty dollars. Got three years in the reform school."

"Conduct many sheriff's sales?"

"No, farm prices are good, so I haven't had many foreclosure sales."

"Good," said his father. "Hate to see good people fail."

"Well, Thomas. You be careful," said his sister, Nettie, eavesdropping from the doorway. "Say, now that George is married, I'm wondering, how about you? Aren't there any good Republican women in Kidder County?"

"Don't believe so, but then I haven't been looking too hard," said Tom, laughing. "But I'm starving. When do we eat?"

Resignation

I knew my grandmother, Adria, had quit her job to marry—a normal practice for the time—but I never heard the particulars. Upon researching the archives of local newspapers, I discovered fascinating articles about my Price grandparents, who had been public figures in their community. It is easy to imagine how the locals might have reacted to those events.

It was a sunny day in May, 1919. Two local women were shopping at the general store in Steele. The benches around the coal stove sat nearly empty, as the farmers were busy in their fields, starting the spring planting of wheat and barley. The pungent smells of cured ham and dill pickles mingled in the air, but Olga, wearing her worn, blue dress, didn't have groceries on her mind. She spread out two bolts of colorful cotton fabric, trying to select a calico print.

Olga hailed her friend. "Sarah! Glad you're here." She pointed to the bolts of fabric. "I'm sewing a dress for the dance Saturday night. I like this light blue print. Still, I'm fond of this cheery red and yellow one. What do you think?"

"The bright one," said Sarah, fashionably dressed in a navy skirt and white blouse. Sarah moved in closer and lowered her voice. "Olga, have you heard? Miss Williams resigned as superintendent yesterday."

"No! You're joking," said Olga, putting down the fabric and giving Sarah her full attention.

"Nope, she just up and quit. News caught 'em by surprise at the county supervisors' board meeting. Miss Williams handed them a written resignation. It stated she wanted to quit as soon as they could find a replacement."

"Why would she quit?"

"All she'd say is 'personal reasons.'"

"Do tell. Is she ill? How about her mother, Mary? She alright?"

"I think so," said Sarah. "Haven't heard of anyone in the Williams family doctoring."

"Well," Olga said, "I noticed on Sunday in church that Miss Williams looked tired. She's been traveling all over the county visiting schools now that the muddy roads have dried. She's got to visit ninety country schools. Maybe the job is too much for her."

"Doubt it. She liked it enough to run for a second term last November. Wouldn't have run if she couldn't handle it."

"True. Maybe someone is giving her a hard time."

Sarah shook her head. "Haven't heard of any feuding."

"People call her progressive, but that's a good thing. She's strict about teacher training and expects them to improve their education," said Olga.

"The only friction I've heard was over attendance. Maybe she's frustrated. Maybe that's the reason she's quitting," said Sarah.

"Hope not. I think she's right. We should enforce attendance rules. Schooling is important today. Miss Williams tried to help by starting the fall session after harvest, so more farm children could attend," noted Olga. "Who'll be taking over?"

"I think Professor Torvend, our city school superintendent. They'll need someone to administer the final exams before the end of May."

At that moment the biggest town gossip, Mr. Brown, entered the store, spotted the ladies in the fabric section, and briskly headed toward them. Seeing the slight, retired bookkeeper approaching, Olga leaned forward and whispered, "He always knows what's going on."

"Hello, Mrs. Smith, Mrs. Hanson," the well-dressed bachelor said, tipping his derby hat and adjusting his wire spectacles. "Have you heard about Miss Williams quitting?" He began fidgeting with the gold watch chain dangling from his vest pocket.

"Yes, we're just talking about her. What happened?"

Brown eagerly shared the latest tidbit. "The board asked Torvend to take over. But I heard it, from a good source, mind you, that he turned it down this morning. I just came from the post office. The board next asked Miss Hildebrand," he said.

"The postmaster's assistant? Is she qualified?"

"Guess so. The law says the superintendent must be a college graduate with a second grade teacher's certificate and have teaching experience in the state. It's certainly a very good paying job. Miss Williams earns $1,500 each year. That's a lot of money for a lady."

"Yes. Any idea why Miss Williams quit so suddenly?" asked Olga.

"Nope … lots of speculation, though. Somebody saw her make a withdrawal from the bank yesterday. Must be planning something. Her family won't talk, either. Why, her mother was downright rude to me this morning, and I was just trying to be friendly," he said shaking his head.

The two women made eye contact, suppressing a laugh.

"Maybe I can find her brother, Edward. Gotta go. Just on my way to the train depot. Heard Miss Williams sat next to the ticket agent during dinner at the hotel." Brown consulted his pocket watch. "He should be back by now. See what I can find out. Good day, ladies."

Turning on his heel, Mr. Brown excused himself without glancing at the store full of dry goods. The ladies giggled as they watched the thin, intense little man rush off on his rounds of every business in town, determined to get to the bottom of Adria Williams' resignation.

"Bet that isn't the last we'll hear from him," Sarah said as she turned in the direction of the women's millinery display.

"Nope, but while he's busy pumping everyone for information, I've got to go." She gathered up the colorful bolt and turned toward the notions counter to select thread. "This pretty red and yellow flower print reminds me of spring," said Olga. Then a thought struck her. "Maybe Miss Williams has a beau. If someone courted me, I'd sure try to keep it a secret in this town, if such a thing is possible."

Once Mr. Brown heard Miss Williams left Steele by train, gossip reached a crescendo. When pressed, the agent confirmed she was ticketed all the way to San Francisco, California. Her mother and brothers refused to comment.

"Why would she go all the way to California on her own?" Mr. Brown wondered aloud making the rounds of businesses. "Does she have relatives there?" No one seemed to know.

Newspaper accounts revealed that the following week a telegram arrived at the newspaper office in Steele, announcing that Thomas Price and Adria Williams were married in Los Angeles, California, on May 15, 1919. The newspaper editor ran the marriage announcement under the headline, "Another Surprise."

Adria did indeed have a beau. It was none other than former Kidder County Sheriff Tom Price, who had completed his second term in December and returned to farming. He had been in California visiting his brother, Frank (Frances).

People knew the two county officials had worked next door to each other in the courthouse, but the public didn't consider them a couple. At the hotel where both Tom and Adria had lived, other guests did not link them romantically. People viewed Tom as a confirmed, middle-aged bachelor. He was still single at forty-nine. No one anticipated he'd marry. Adria, like her predecessor, was expected to remain a spinster. She was college-educated and financially independent, rare for a woman—perhaps she intimidated potential suitors. At thirty-seven, Adria was well beyond the usual marrying age. She hadn't appeared interested in looking for a man. She dressed conservatively, perhaps a bit dowdy. No higher hemlines for her. She showed no interest in the latest fashions or hairstyles. Although attractive and pleasant, Adria was a bit heavy for her five-foot three-inch frame.

Adria had grown up with four brothers and felt at ease conducting business with men. She quietly but firmly held her own, earning the respect of men on the local school boards she supervised. Unafraid to take a stand on issues she believed in, her manner was dignified, with an easy, contagious laugh. Adria never forgot she was in the public eye and tried to remain proper and above reproach.

Printed wedding announcements for their family and friends soon arrived. These were strictly a formality, as everyone in Steele, and most of the county, had heard about the marriage. Having lived in a rural community, I consider it amazing that Tom and Adria had managed to keep their relationship secret from prying eyes. That was no small accomplishment.

A few of their friends claimed they'd known all along the two officials had been "an item," but had respected their wishes and kept their relationship confidential. The Steele paper quoted Arnie Vinje, one of Tom's closest friends, as exclaiming, "No surprise there. They've been engaged for two years!"

Nosy Mr. Brown felt compelled to get to the bottom of the story. He practically snorted at his neighbor in the local pool hall. "No way they've been courtin' for two years. Don't believe a word of it." Brown was clearly upset that this match happened right under his nose.

◆   ◆   ◆

When the couple decided to remain in California after the marriage, Tom returned alone to North Dakota to sell part of his farm. He kept part of his land and Adria's homestead land and arranged to have it farmed on shares. Besides providing income from the grain, his land had the potential for oil or other minerals that were rumored to be present. Land served as his safety net.

Before returning to his wife, he also visited his parents and siblings in South Dakota. "You're going to be grandparents again," he told them. What he didn't mention was that the baby was due in a couple weeks.

Tom and Adria made the difficult decision to keep the birth of their first child secret until an appropriate time had elapsed since their May wedding.

In their public positions they had been enforcers of morality. As sheriff, Tom had been called on to arrest people for "cohabitation" or "bastardly conduct." As supervisor of county teachers, Adria had no choice but to dismiss any teacher under her jurisdiction who was single and pregnant. If she had stayed on in her role as Kidder County Superintendent of Schools, though she had married, she undoubtedly would have been fired in disgrace for her early pregnancy, although she had an otherwise flawless record. Both Tom and Adria had been set on pedestals as public role models. They chose to leave town rather than endure public ridicule and sully their reputations. The newlyweds settled down into private life in Los Angeles County.

Tom was approached to join the Los Angeles Police Department, but he told Adria he "didn't have the stomach for it." He had followed newspaper accounts of departmental scandal and probably thought a straight arrow like himself might not fit in. Or maybe he knew he had grown too old for police work.

Tom returned to Los Angeles just days before Adria delivered a healthy baby girl on September 13, 1919. They named her Harriet Pearl after her maternal grandmother. Their curly-haired daughter inherited her father's blue eyes, and they both adored her. Surprised at becoming a parent, Adria settled into full-time motherhood. As a progressive woman advocating women's suffrage, she must have had a huge adjustment in giving up the responsibility and authority she previously enjoyed in her career.

The couple shared their good news with their new California neighbors, but they waited to tell their families back in the Dakotas. With no phone calls or visits back and forth within the family, only letters or telegrams, a baby was easy to conceal.

Tom and Adria settled in the rapidly growing new community of Hawthorne, south of Los Angeles. In 1920, they purchased two new adjacent houses each with double lots, living in one house and renting the second. The main terminus for the Los Angeles Railway line was located just blocks from their new home, so Tom became a streetcar conductor. "Instead of carrying people around in a wagon and horses or driving them in a Model T," he declared, "I'll drive them in a street car on electric tracks."

Besides the house rental, they received income from their rented wheat lands in North Dakota. The couple further augmented their income by raising chickens in their back yard and selling eggs to local markets.

On February 12, 1920, Tom and Adria sent telegrams to Dakota relatives. "Healthy daughter," they declared. Belatedly, the Prices announced the arrival of their first-born daughter to the families back home. They used her middle name, Pearl, and always celebrated her birthday in February.

A year later, the couple told their family Adria was again expecting. My father, Bruce Arthur, was born October 14, 1921. At age fifty-two, Tom had a son, probably feeling more like a grandfather than a father. Tom wondered if he'd be around to see his son grown.

◆   ◆   ◆

Bruce and Pearl Price.

The Prices didn't drive back to the Dakotas until 1923. By then Bruce had turned two and Pearl was a precocious toddler of three-and-a-half, although actually she was four.

Tom and his family rented out their second California house and remained in North Dakota for six years. They visited Adria's family in Steele, and Polly Price, Tom's mother, in Aberdeen, SD. His father, Daniel, had died a year earlier.

Tom was devastated that he hadn't had an opportunity to pay his respects at the time of his father's death. On August 30, 1922, Daniel's family had sent a telegram to Tom in Inglewood, California, but it was misdirected to Englewood, Colorado. By the time Tom learned of his father's death, the funeral was over and his siblings had returned to their homes around the country. Tom's father never met Adria or the children. After returning to the Dakotas, Tom visited his dear mother several times before she passed away in 1925. At eighty-nine years old, Polly died of pneumonia during one of his visits.

Tom and Adria stayed in Steele near Adria's mother, Mary Williams, for a short time, giving her a chance to get acquainted with her grandchildren. Since her divorce, Mary was negative toward all men, including her new son-in-law. Considering Mary's judgmental nature, it seems unlikely Mary ever learned of her daughter's secret. Perhaps the only person Adria may have confided in about the early pregnancy was her brother, Spencer, a Presbyterian pastor.

The Prices moved back to their old farm come spring, their secret safe.

Gunder and Maren Sjøli, Maternal Great-Grandparents: Norwegians Come to America

Maren and Gunder Sjøli, Great-grandparents.

In the 1860s, Norway offered little opportunity for Gunder, my maternal great-grandfather. Norway's agricultural economy could no longer sustain its growing population, so many of its young people left their homeland for America.

Born in 1840, Gunder had been raised on the Sjøli farm in Hedmark County, Norway, north of Kongsvinger, the youngest of eleven children. Tradition dictated that the eldest son (or daughter if no sons survived) inherited the land. The rest of the sons could only become cotters (tenant farmers) or leave the land. Although he yearned to farm, Gunder studied with a tailor and became quite skilled.

A stocky young man with a full beard, Gunder married a neighbor girl, Maren, and they moved in with her parents for a time. They all attended the Brandval Church near both family farms. The young couple lost their first son at birth, but two years later had a healthy daughter.

In 1867, Gunder brought his wife and infant to America. The young family lived in a Norwegian farm settlement in Iowa, where Gunder labored on a farm by day and toiled into the night as a tailor, sewing men's suits and coats by hand.

The couple used Gunder's surname, Olson or Olsen, based on the Norwegian tradition of patronymics, of using the father's given name for the child's surname. (i.e., Gunder was the son of Ole, thus Olsen; Maren's father's name was Amund Eriksen Hofoss, thus her maiden surname, Amundsdatter.) The farm where they lived often provided the third name (i.e., Sjøli for Gunder and Hanestadmoen for Maren). Spellings varied even within families.

Tailoring proved lucrative in their newly adopted country. Gunder later told his grandchildren he'd brought nearly $9000 worth of twenty-dollar gold pieces when they moved farther westward from Iowa into Minnesota. He successfully concealed the small fortune in two-gallon pails, using part of the money to purchase oxen, a wagon, and farming supplies.

He joined ten other Norwegian families in settling newly available homesteading lands in Ottertail County, Minnesota, in 1870. His homestead consisted of lakes and grassland, different from Norway in that his new home had little timber. About five years later, he took his oath of American citizenship as Gunder Olson Sjollie. He had dropped the Olson patronymic, perhaps to avoid confusion with too many Olson families. Official documents used spelling variants of their place of origin, Sjøli, which eventually became Anglicized to a close-sounding approximate, Shirley. He was known as Gunder Shirley the rest of his life.

◆   ◆   ◆

Although the Sioux had been removed to reservations, small bands of Native Americans, probably Cheyenne, still frequently passed through the little farming community on hunting trips. They didn't bother the white settlers. The immigrants wisely gave the natives a wide berth and let them take whatever food they needed. The newly minted Americans maintained a mutual suspicion of the natives, aware of violent outbreaks in other Minnesota farming settlements just eight years earlier.

One day Maren had just returned home from baking several loaves of bread in her neighbor's oven, four miles away. Tired after walking the round trip, Maren looked up from her stove to observe several Indians quietly walking into her homestead shack. They helped themselves to the freshly baked bread on the kitchen table, leaving one loaf for the family, then left without a word. This upset Maren, but of course she couldn't confront the strangers.

As soon as they were gone, she ran to the barn and reported the visit to her husband, assuring him the family was fine: "Gunder, they didn't trouble us, but they took my bread. All I have left is enough bread for one meal."

Maren soon got her own oven.

Gunder acted civilly towards the Indian travelers that passed through Ottertail County. The two groups sometimes had to set aside their differences, especially in inclement weather, to survive the elements. The most unsettling encounter happened on a frigid winter night when two Indians on foot sought shelter. Gunder allowed them to spend the night, but slept on the floor nearby with his saber, just in case. The Indians, grateful to sleep indoors, continued peacefully on their way by daylight.

On September 30, 1884, Gunder became a proud landowner, officially granted a homestead parcel of 153.5 acres. He understood gold could be spent, but land lasted forever, the true measure of a man's wealth. Gunder's golden nest egg, plus backbreaking work, allowed the Shirleys to build a thriving wheat and dairy farm where they raised nine children.

My grandfather, Gustav or Gust, was their seventh child, born April 8, 1879. The children attended the local country school and the South Immanuel Lutheran church, which Gunder helped build. Gust, brown-haired and blue-eyed, grew to medium height with a stocky, athletic build. He was in demand as a softball pitcher.

A devout Lutheran, Gunder hoped one of his sons would choose to attend a Lutheran seminary and become a pastor. But, like their father, they wanted to farm. So Gunder financed the pastoral education for a neighbor's son.

Gust married a pretty Norwegian neighbor girl, Othilda Weik, in 1900. That December they had a healthy son whom they named Arthur, a name popularized by President Chester A. Arthur. They adopted the American tradition of selecting given names for their children rather than naming them after relatives in a prescribed pattern. They soon added two daughters, Minnie and Gladys.

Around this time Gust and his brothers looked westward for land of their own, much as their father had done a generation earlier. In 1905, Gunder reportedly gave his three sons, Carl, Olaf, and Gust, his blessings and $4,000 each for start-up money to help them get established on farms of their own. "This will help you get started homesteading in North Dakota," Gunder said with great satisfaction. Then he admonished them, "Use it wisely."

By 1910, America's farmland had been nearly all settled. Those three sons became my family's last generation of American homesteaders. Gunder's daughters were expected to marry, while the youngest son, Martin, inherited the Minnesota farm in exchange for providing a home for his aging parents.

Gunder continued to supplement his farming income by hand-tailoring men's suits by lantern light until he was blinded by cataracts. He scheduled eye surgery, still experimental in the 1920s, but at the last minute cancelled, fearing the operation. Gunder spent his remaining years blind, living with his youngest son's family.

On one of his last trips to visit his aging father, Gust brought along some of Gunder's grandchildren. Hilda described to me how Gunder asked the children to present themselves, one at a time, so he could touch them to discern their height and build. His deft but wrinkled fingers then gently traced their youthful hands and faces as he tried to picture them.

Maren died at seventy and Gunder at eighty-nine. Their homestead in Ottertail County, Minnesota, remains in the family.

Gustav Shirley, Maternal Grandfather.

Gustav Shirley, Maternal Grandfather: Dakota Homesteader

Seeking homestead land, Gust, his brothers, and their families traveled westward. They headed for the newly surveyed lands in North Dakota during the railroad-sponsored boom of 1905-06. Several neighboring families from Ottertail County, Minnesota, moved with them—the nucleus of a new Norwegian community.

Gust didn't use oxen and wagon for the trek westward, as his father had a generation earlier. He purchased bargain tickets on the highly advertised Northern Pacific Railroad to reach his destination in Dawson, North Dakota. The Shirleys shipped their possessions in a freight boxcar on the same train, including farm animals, implements, and machinery. They even brought along the kids' pet dog, Fido.

Excitement built at the railway station as the children raced up the steps of the wooden platform. Soon the families settled inside one of the passenger cars on the noisy, steam-powered train. The swaying cars lurched forward, nearly knocking over the smallest travelers, while the shrill parting whistle signaled the beginning of their two-hundred-mile journey to a new home.

While the children explored the passenger car, the ladies lingered at the windows, tearfully waving at relatives left behind. What would their new life bring? Would they ever see their Minnesota friends and relatives again?

The women soon noticed, with some apprehension, fewer lakes, rivers, and trees rolling by the windows. The landscape turned flat as they crossed the Red River at the North Dakota border. Soon the land became a drift prairie ridge with rolling grasslands as they traveled to Kidder County, in the middle of the state. To the west flowed the Missouri River, where the Lewis and Clark expedition had wintered in the Mandan Indian village a hundred years earlier. The great river divided the wetter eastern portion of the state from the drier west, where beef cattle ranches would outnumber farmers.

The men recognized the terrain. They had made a similar trip the preceding fall, going ahead to select homestead sites and file the paperwork before returning to their Minnesota home. Now they moved their families and possessions in time for spring planting. Arriving in the railroad hub of Dawson, Gust's family transferred to horse and wagon and headed northward to their homestead, a bumpy twenty-four-mile ride. Using surveying markers, they found the land Gust had chosen. They only carried their clothes, bedding, food, and a few cooking utensils.

Bachelors in the group stayed behind in Dawson, arranging transport of the larger items by horse and cart. Then they herded the settlers' stock northward. The travelers observed mile upon mile of nothingness, populated only with plentiful birds and small game. The unending sea of grasslands swayed in the wind, with thousands of acres ready for cultivation, a clean canvas on which to build a new farming community.

Tribes of the Sioux Nation, who for generations had passed through this region when hunting, had recently been rounded up and confined to distant reservations. They'd left the land as they found it, with only arrowheads or an occasional rock fire circle as evidence. The buffalo were nearly extinct—even their bones had been picked up and sold years ago by the earliest explorers. The land itself probably looked the same in 1905 as it had in 1805.

The Norwegian pioneers passed Horsehead Lake, named for its shape, and numerous wetland sloughs, but found no trees or rivers. The discussion turned to finding well water, essential for survival. "Sure hope we'll hit a vein of water close to where we build," Gust said.

Occasionally they saw a crude wood and tarpaper shack. Finally, as they neared their destination, they spotted more homestead shacks, a mile or two apart, dotting the countryside. One belonged to my paternal grandfather, Tom Price, Gust's neighbor.

Othilda Weik Shirley, Gust's first wife.

Othilda's brother, Oscar Weik, Gust, Othilda, and their four children by
their new home.

♦　　♦　　♦

Gust, his wife, Othilda, and their three children, Art, four, Minnie, two,
and Gladys, a few months old, lived in a tent while they chose the farm site
and built a homestead shack. "Now if we find good water, we'll be set," Gust
noted as he studied the rolling countryside.

They had brought along chickens that ranged nearby until they could build
a chicken coop to contain them. Othilda asked her preschool children to look
for eggs in the tall green grass. They discovered two eggs in a makeshift nest but
impulsively did their own cooking, mud-pie style. They happily created fancy
cakes and pies bound together by the raw egg whites, until their father caught
them. Gust had noticed empty eggshells behind the tent and administered a
spanking and a lecture about squandering the precious eggs. The family ate no
eggs that day.

Gust and Othilda planted potatoes, a main staple in their diet. They
discovered, to their delight, that potatoes were especially well suited to the
sandy loam soil. In later years Gust often sold farmers his remaining stockpile
of potatoes for seed the next spring. The whole potatoes were simply cut

into sections leaving at least one eye, or undeveloped bud, in each section, and planted by hand in rows. "We always plant enough potatoes," Gust said. "Can't imagine why anyone would run out of potatoes. Just poor planning."

Gust, standing center, supervising sodbusting on his homestead.

Gust dug a well and gave thanks when he reached plentiful water. He had enough cash to hire a huge tractor for his sodbusting, rather than use horses. For the next few years they lived frugally in the simple wooden shack while Gust broke more land to the plow and constructed farm buildings.

Gust splurged on a car. He may well have owned the first auto in the area. His 1905 Studebaker arrived by rail in Steele. Using its owner's manual, Gust managed to get the car started and get it in gear. Once underway, Gust realized that he didn't know how to stop the new invention. While he was probably driving less than ten miles per hour, he panicked and opted to drive it into a tree. The impact bent the front axle, requiring major repairs.

In 1908, a fourth child, Gilma, was born. A year later, Gust constructed a fine two-story farmhouse. He then recycled the homesteading shack as an animal shed. Eventually he added additional rooms to the house and built a big front porch, the envy of neighbors who hadn't done as well.

Meanwhile, the newcomers had quickly organized a Lutheran congregation and social clubs like those back in Minnesota. The settlers placed a high priority on religion. They lived their faith, looking after one another, literally becoming their brothers' keepers. The families worshiped, when they could, with an itinerant minister, and the Ladies Aid became the backbone of social activities. Meetings usually included whole families who ate picnic-style and played ball games at the hosting farm. Gust, strong, with a good pitching arm, remained in demand as a softball pitcher. He was thankful that softball teams formed quickly in his new home.

Each spring and fall the congregation held Sunday School classes. Families especially anticipated the Sunday School Christmas presentations. The ladies sold meals, baked goods, and colorful quilts, along with delicate embroidery fancywork. This raised money for the pastor's salary and the long-anticipated new church building.

As soon as it was feasible, Gust and his Norwegian neighbors built a Lutheran church strikingly similar to their former church in Ottertail County, Minnesota. The transplanted church carpenter, Isaac Seele, had carried the architectural plans in his head. The white clapboard two-story building featured a steep roof, tall enough to add balcony seating if the congregation grew larger. The two longer sides of the rectangular building featured four arch-shaped plain-glass windows. A tall bell tower rose from the front of the church to a tapered, wood-shingled steeple that could be seen for miles across the prairie, a beacon of refuge. It stood until 1950, when the steeple was removed due to weather damage. While the tall grain elevators were the economic heart of the community, its churches (Lutheran and Methodist) were the spiritual and social centers.

Bethany Lutheran Church ninety years after founding

The pioneers included a basement to house Sunday School classes and church suppers. The Lutheran congregation proudly opened its doors in 1916, with services in both Norwegian and English.

◆   ◆   ◆

Gust's hard work paid off. Times were booming for the first two decades of the century. Gust planted wheat and barley, raised beef cattle and hogs, and milked dairy cows while demand for farm products remained high. With ample rain and good prices, prosperity reigned. The years 1900-1920, later called the Golden Age of Agriculture, proved the best of times for Gust.

Not all the pioneers succeeded at farming, however. Some lacked ambition, physical or management skills, or simply suffered bad luck. Many neighbors struggled. One crisp autumn morning, a less affluent neighbor stopped by as Gust checked four curing hams hanging from the rafters in a farm shed.

"What you gonna do with all that pork?" the neighbor asked enviously.

"Eat it," Gust replied. "That's why I've been fattening up those pigs all summer. Gotta plan ahead for winter."

"Sure wish I had a pig to butcher," the neighbor said before departing.

Early the next morning Gust again checked on his curing hams. His mouth dropped open, and he stared in disbelief. One ham was missing.

With no sign of break-in by animals, Gust guessed what might have happened. He had often helped this particular neighbor by giving him potatoes and garden vegetables, but this was betrayal, outright stealing from a neighbor, the worst kind of thievery.

Gust immediately headed off on foot across the pasture to the neighbor's farm and marched into their house, without knocking. Sure enough, he found the family just sitting down to a big breakfast. A familiar looking ham, tied with Gust's unique twine, sat on the sideboard, intact except for a few missing slices.

The neighbor, caught red-handed, stood speechless. Gust strode over to inspect the ham and then approached his neighbor, stopping to look him square in the eyes. Without uttering a word, Gust turned on his heel and stomped off.

If Gust had reported the crime to the county sheriff, the thief might have been jailed. Social ostracism seemed the better option. Gust later explained his decision to his children, "If he's in jail, those kids might go hungry."

The following morning the fourth ham, with one small section missing, had been returned to the shed. The two men never spoke to each other about the incident, but of course word spread.

Just when life became financially easier, Gust's twenty-nine-year-old wife, Othilda, fell ill with tuberculosis and could no longer care for their four children, now ranging in age from two to nine. Anxious to stay on the farm and keep his family together, Gust looked for domestic help.

Petra Hanson, Maternal Grandmother.

Petra Hanson, Maternal Grandmother: Babies and Baking

Thirty-year-old Gustav Shirley had reached a turning point. His stricken wife, Othilda, was failing. Early in 1910, Gust hired Petra Hanson, a never-married immigrant from Modum, Norway, to care for his dying wife and four young children, Arthur, Minnie, Gladys, and Gilma. Norwegian friends had recommended the thirty-year-old woman living nearby who had worked as a domestic and telephone operator in Norway. There were no job opportunities in North Dakota, though, for a telephone operator who didn't speak English. Petra never owned a phone during her life in America.

Petra contracted to work for Gust via letter. Her work agreement provided food, lodging, and a small salary. Gust dispatched his nine-year-old son, Arthur, to bring Petra to the Shirley household from ten miles away by horse and wagon.

Petra settled into Gust's new farmhouse, which had no plumbing, but was luxurious by prairie standards. Many of their neighbors were still living in homestead shacks. Strong, quiet, and accustomed to hard toil from an early age, Petra found plenty of work to earn her keep. Gust's first question to her was, "Can you cook?" She answered a simple, "Yes," and soon proved it in the kitchen. She quickly earned a reputation as an excellent cook. Meanwhile, she began learning English.

Othilda Shirley grew steadily weaker. She lost her battle with tuberculosis and died June 10, 1910. The young mother was one of the earliest burials in the new Lutheran cemetery, a half-mile from Gust's farm, on land donated two years earlier by Othilda's brother, Oscar Weik. Gust, the volunteer caretaker of the cemetery, continued in that role for some thirty-five years.

After burying Othilda, Gust asked Petra to stay on for a while. "I want to keep the children together. Need someone to care for them while I'm in the fields," he told her.

"Yah, I will," Petra said, nodding in agreement, although gossips questioned the propriety of the arrangement.

At their mother's wake, Minnie, seven, and Gladys, five, both wearing their calico Sunday School dresses, overhead the Norwegian Ladies Aid women on the front porch talking about the girls' future. "Do you think Gust can keep the family together?" someone asked. "Young Arthur can get by with his father, but Gust can't farm and take care of three little girls. Maybe it would be better to adopt them out. Both Gust and Othilda have relatives here. Surely, someone could take them."

The wide-eyed girls panicked as they overhead the conversation. Another neighbor continued, "Maybe Gust can afford to hire Miss Hanson to stay on. Is she good with children?"

"Believe so. They seem well cared for."

Little Gladys, near tears and clinging to her older sister, whispered, "These ladies want to take us away. I wanna stay here. I want Mama."

The ladies noticed the girls and beckoned to them. "Gladys, come here. Don't be shy. Is Miss Hanson mean to you?" Gladys shuffled forward looking down at her only shoes. She said nothing, too bashful to speak.

"Minnie, how about you. Can you tell us, how does Miss Hanson treat you?"

"She makes me work hard."

"Good. Everyone must do her share. Does she ever beat you?"

"Oh, no. Sometimes Pa does. With his razor strap." The neighbor lady nodded in approval. Spanking was the norm in the "spare the rod and spoil the child" era.

"Well, we'll just keep an eye on things."

Gust marked the customary six-month bereavement period quietly, keeping busy with his farming. Soon, however, Petra's short-term work agreement evolved into a long-term, loving relationship. She and Gust quietly married at the Lutheran parsonage on March 9, 1911. Petra became a stepmother, knowing full well she could never replace the older children's biological mother or Gust's first love. He left his first marriage certificate hanging on the wall.

Six months later, she and Gust had the first of their nine children together, all within a span of thirteen years. As in Gust's first marriage, the first baby came a little early. The community quit whispering and accepted them as a couple. Gust's thirteen kids were viewed as just another large family, welcome hands to help on the farm.

◆   ◆   ◆

Petra could personally identify with the pain and upheaval caused by the early loss of a parent. Back in Buskerud County, Norway, her father, Hans Berntsen, fell ill and died when Petra was thirteen. The loss of the family breadwinner signaled the end of Petra's childhood.

Nils Mikkelsen, Petra's stepfather.

Petra's father had worked as a *"husmann,"* or tenant farm laborer. His widow, Lise, and her seven children faced dire financial straits. Although the young widow likely received help from her own father who lived nearby, she needed a husband to survive financially. Although Petra didn't speak of this difficult time in her life, as the eldest, she probably assumed some of the burden of earning money for food along with her brother, Brent, eleven.

The widowed Lise must have been flattered when she caught the eye of Nils Mikkelsen, a strong and ruggedly handsome lumberjack with broad shoulders and a heavy beard. Seemingly well off, Nils lived near Modum, Norway. He'd already "seen the world" in Lise's estimation, having traveled to America some twenty years earlier. Still youthful at fifty, Nils had returned from homesteading in the United States and held American citizenship. He bragged of America and its unlimited grassland ready for the taking. Such big talk must have sounded enticing to Lise and her three older boys, who saw no economic future in Norway.

Throughout their lives, Lise and her children had been devout Lutherans, but Nils didn't enjoy good standing with the Norwegian state church during this time, perhaps because of an earlier divorce granted for deserting his wife in Norway. He listed himself as a religious dissenter on the Norwegian census of 1900.

Lise bore a daughter, Nellie, and a son, Nathan, before Nils married her on November 1, 1900. Church marriage records indicate she was a widow of thirty-seven and he a divorcé of fifty-three, both eligible to remarry in the eyes of the church. Apparently he failed to mention to the clergy—or to his bride—the many children whom he had abandoned on both continents. He concealed this secret throughout his marriage to Lise.

With Nils supporting them, Petra no longer had to worry about food, but the teenager hated the way Nils treated her mother. Her stepfather proved harsh and tight-fisted, withholding money for basic household necessities such as laundry soap, making her mother beg for supplies. Lise was continually exhausted by pregnancy, giving birth to another healthy daughter, Mildred, and then twins who died shortly after birth. Meanwhile, Nils expected young Petra to earn a living and help care for the younger siblings. Loyalty toward her mother probably kept her from moving away.

In March, 1903, the Mikkelsen family (Nils, Lise, and their three children) immigrated to America on the ship, Saxsonia. That November, five of Lise's children by her original marriage (Brent, Johanna, Olga, Paul, and Oscar Hanson) arrived aboard the Ultonia. They took the rails inland, stopped with her relatives in Minnesota, then later settled in Kidder County, North Dakota. Nils and Brent soon filed homesteads.

Two older girls, Caroline and Petra, stayed behind, unable to pay their trans-Atlantic tickets. Caroline arrived next, but my grandmother, Petra, didn't save enough money for passage until 1907. She was the last family member to come to America. Women's wages were low, and at times Petra doubted whether she could ever accumulate enough money to join her family.

Once in America, Petra's brothers became farm laborers. They applied for citizenship and filed for homesteads when they reached twenty-one. Women's jobs, usually working as domestics or laundresses, scarcely paid a living wage, so Petra's three sisters found supporting themselves more difficult. The women, all marriageable age, soon found husbands among the frontier men.

◆   ◆   ◆

Petra's contract with ship and railroad to bring her from Norway to America.

On Sept 28, 1907, Petra embarked on a journey to the new world with a small trunk containing her possessions. Traveling alone, Petra knew her life would change forever. I wonder if she realized that she'd never see her homeland again.

On that crisp September day, the shy, brown-haired, blue-eyed Petra patiently waited in line to show her paperwork to the local chief of police in the presence of the shipping company's representative. She had collected proof of her birth, baptism, and church confirmation, as well as her smallpox vaccination record, from the Lutheran Church of Norway. Her papers were in order; she felt confident she'd pass the required departure physicals, and she'd purchased the one-way ticket. If only she knew English. The police chief bellowed, "*Neste*," (next) as his hand stamp sounded a thud on her "kontrakt," acknowledging a security deposit that Norway demanded from the shipping company. His purple hand-stamp stood vivid against the white paper.

Clutching her contract, her Bible, and photos of home, Petra no doubt looked back one last time upon the only world she had known—the forested mountains and fjords of Norway, including her picturesque Heggen church near the present-day Vikersund ski area. Her brothers had written, describing Dakota as a very different place, nearly flat with tall, lush grass, but little water and no trees. Skis were unneeded in their new home.

Petra survived the crowded voyage aboard the S.S. Ivernia without contracting an illness. On October 10, 1907, she passed the arrival health inspection and stood on American soil in Boston. Language proved her biggest obstacle as she struggled to order lunch.

Twenty-seven-year-old Petra Hanson permanently left the ocean upon arriving in America. Her destination, North Dakota, lies exactly in the middle of the North American continent. She would be living as far from the coasts as physically possible. Never again could she watch the Norwegian fishermen arrive with their catch, hear the pounding waves, or smell the sea. Petra boarded a train and traveled 1500 miles inland.

"*Velkommen* to Amerika," yelled her brothers as they greeted her at the Steele train station. She could hardly contain her joy at seeing her mother and her siblings. She soon moved in with her brothers.

◆   ◆   ◆

The next year on December 19, 1908, Petra's mother, Lise Paulsen Mikkelsen, age forty-five, gave birth to her fourteenth baby, a healthy girl. At first, all went well with mother and child, and then Lise unexpectedly died of complications, probably toxemia or infection. They named the surviving baby "Lisa," spelled the American way, in honor of her mother. The newspaper account of the mother's death reported that the prior day Lise had been up working, seemingly a strong, healthy woman. Suddenly she was gone, leaving a husband and children of all ages, from Petra to the newborn.

After four years of separation, Petra's joyful reunion with her mother in America had proved short-lived, leaving Petra grief-stricken. Coincidently, the same week Lise died, her married adult daughter, Olga, gave birth to twins in the same frontier community. They were Olga's first babies.

When the local ladies arrived at Nils Mikkelsen's farm soon after they heard of his wife's death, they were met with more sad news. "Olga gave birth to twin boys. Born early. One died soon after it came into this world. The other isn't doing so good," said Mrs. Kleve, a close neighbor, as she prepared to bathe and dress the deceased woman for her funeral.

"How sad," replied Mrs. Severson, another neighbor who'd prepared meals for the bereaved family. "How's the new mother doing?"

"She's recovering, but of course she's heartbroken. First her mother dies, and then her newborn son. The second baby is tiny. Might not be able to save him either," said Mrs. Kleve, smoothing her crisp white apron. "Doesn't look good. They're trying to find a doctor now."

A third neighbor lady spoke up, "Did you know Lise and Nils also lost a set of twins before moving here?"

"Yes, she told me. Makes you wonder how much one family can endure."

Mrs. Kleve continued, "We must find a wet nurse for baby Lisa. Perhaps Olga will have enough milk for her and the twin."

"I hope so. She's the only nursing mother close."

The men had just gone to the Kleve cemetery to prepare Lise's grave. Mrs. Severson asked, "Should we send someone to tell them to dig another for the baby? Why don't we bury Lise's grandson with her?"

"Seems fitting. I'll ask the family."

The next day, family and friends gathered on the wind-swept country cemetery to bury the newborn baby boy in the same pine coffin with his grandmother. The gravediggers had expressed relief that it was early enough in the winter that the earth hadn't yet frozen solid. The virgin soil in the graveyard remained undisturbed, except for a couple graves. The settlers didn't have a church or pastor yet, but had already established a place to bury their dead.

Most of Lise's children attended. Barrel-chested Nils stood stoically graveside, surrounded by his youngest children. Bundled against the cold wind, they watched with teary eyes and red, drippy noses.

Later in the week the same neighbors built a tiny casket and dug another grave for the second twin. The grieving parents of the twins, Olga and Hogan Mallengen, adopted Lise's surviving baby girl (who was Olga's half sister) and raised her as their own. They later nicknamed her Lizzie.

Meanwhile, the widower, Nils, decided he couldn't care for his remaining children. He kept the eldest son, Nathan, with him to work on the farm for a year until he could prove up and win possession of the homestead. Nellie, Mildred, and Olaf were parceled out among various friends and neighbors, a fate not uncommon for motherless children. The oldest, ten-year-old Nellie, went to live with an aunt and uncle in Minnesota, while a neighbor temporarily took little Olaf. A childless couple, Caroline and Ole Haugen, living five miles away, adopted Mildred. Lise's children (Petra's siblings) scattered throughout Minnesota and North Dakota, seldom seeing one another. Petra again found herself largely on her own, this time in America, her adopted land.

As soon as Nils earned the patent on his homestead in October of 1910, he sold the land and returned to Norway permanently, taking only his youngest son, Olaf. Nathan, now ten, who had been living with his father on the homestead, stayed in America and joined his sister, Mildred. Both grew to adulthood with their adoptive parents. The children remaining behind in North Dakota never heard from or saw their father again.

Documentation remains sketchy, but it shows Nils apparently had fourteen children and at least three wives in overlapping marriages, on two continents. Nils farmed in Wisconsin and homesteaded in both South Dakota and North Dakota, using different names—Mikkelsen and Lundy. He made several trips between America and Norway, dying in his homeland in 1925 at age seventy-eight.

His past came to light when Mildred Mikkelsen, a daughter of Nils and Lise, met Gabriele Lundy, a son from Nils' marriage to Gunhild Syversdatter. The two compared photos and confirmed they had the same absent father.

Gust Shirley family 1926. From back left: Gilma, Art, Petra, Gust, Orville, Agnes, Minnie, Gladys, front: Hilda, Edna, Evelyn, Edwin, Glen, Gilbert, and Melvin.

The Brief Golden Years

Back in North Dakota, Petra and Gust Shirley expanded their family. Petra gave birth to nine healthy babies. Gust and Petra named their children Hilda, Orville, Agnes, Melvin, Gilbert, Edna, Edwin, Glen, and Evelyn.

I can only imagine Petra's mixed feelings regarding the later pregnancies, considering her own mother died in late-in-life childbirth. Although both were strong women, birthing babies into their mid-forties had to be difficult. I marvel at their stamina and fortitude.

All thirteen of the Shirley children were educated in the local grammar schools, which involved considerable hardship when traveling to school during harsh winter weather. Art bragged of carrying his younger sister, Minnie, on his back when the snowdrifts became too deep for her to navigate.

Higher education was a different matter. Birth order as well as the family's changing economic fortunes dictated the educational levels of the Shirley clan. The two eldest, Minnie and Arthur, dropped out after grade school because they were needed to work full-time at home, a typical practice among pioneers.

Between 1910 and the middle 1920s, Gust established himself farming, and good markets for wheat made farming profitable for a time. Several of his sons and daughters finished high school, with three daughters completing teacher's training. He began a practice he couldn't maintain when he gave land to his oldest son.

Using a short-lived health problem as an excuse, Gust didn't permit his last daughter, Evelyn, to attend high school. In reality she was needed at home to help her aging mother. The younger sons also stayed home during their teen years to farm for their father. Decades later, Evelyn wrote an equivalency test to secure the long-coveted diploma.

◆　　　◆　　　◆

All too soon, drought and depressed grain and beef prices changed family fortunes. It was 1931 on the Shirley farm.

"Where are Glen and Evelyn?" Petra asked after looking at the kitchen clock. "It's time for their baths."

"They're south of the barn, snaring gophers," answered her twelve-year-old daughter, Edna. "Evelyn's helping Glen set the snares. Glen's been carrying around Dad's old tobacco pouch stuffed full of gopher tails."

The pesky rodents created havoc for farmers, digging holes and eating vegetation. The county government tried to reduce their numbers by offering penny-a-tail bounties.

"Edna, go get your brother and sister. The bath water is almost heated," Petra said as she finished peeling potatoes for the evening meal and dried her hands on her full white apron. She then used hot pads to pull rhubarb pies from the oven for Sunday dinner.

"Where will they spend the money?" asked Edna.

"They'll probably buy candy. Why don't you earn some money?"

"Killing those poor little gophers! Yuck," Edna said making a face. "I'm not going to sit all day waiting for a gopher to pop his ugly head up from his hole. Then I'd have to lasso him with a piece of twine. I'd still have to hit 'em on the head to kill 'em. Glen can do that, but I can't even drown one."

"Then quit complaining. Now go fetch those two so we can start baths," Petra said firmly as she set out a brush for Evelyn's blonde hair.

The big aluminum tub sat waiting in a corner of the kitchen. Clean clothes and a stack of towels rested on the kitchen chairs arranged for privacy in front of the tub. Saturday afternoon on the Shirley farm meant it was time to get everyone fed, bathed, and dressed for going to Robinson.

Gust typically traded eighteen dozen eggs and five gallons of cream for food and sundries at Swanson's Store. If he purchased more than their value, the difference would be added to his monthly store tab. Gust prided himself on paying the tab on time each month. In exchange for being a valued customer, the grocer would include a bag of hard candy. Petra kept the candy in her dresser drawer and used it to reward the children.

A couple hours later, Gust had cleaned up after downing an early dinner of fried ham, corn, and potatoes. He asked, "Is the grocery list ready?"

"Yes, Pa, I'm adding black embroidery floss to the list like Ma told me," replied Edna.

"Swanson expects to have some peaches this week. I'll get a lug if they're sweet," Gust told Petra. As usual she would have to can them Sunday because they were highly perishable.

"Everyone who's going to town, get in the car," announced Gust.

The kitchen quickly emptied. Each youngster looked forward to seeing friends and spending the coin their father gave them at the local store's candy counter. The older ones danced at Wick's Dance Hall, with the younger ones looking on. After doing the family trading, Gust would join his buddies in the bar for a few drinks.

Relieved that seven-year-old Evelyn, her last child, was old enough to go with her siblings, Petra savored an evening alone. After getting everyone off to town, fifty-one-year-old Petra would bathe herself. She'd shampoo and braid her long white hair and finally relax with her favorite *Decorah-Posten* weekly newspaper, written in her native Norwegian. Her one luxury was a quiet Saturday evening after seven days of backbreaking work.

Petra rarely went anywhere, even church. Although a person of strong faith, Petra said she needed rest more than she needed to attend church services. She preferred reading her well-worn Norwegian Bible at home.

Petra's good navy dress hung in the closet ready for special occasions, but she was usually too shy or too busy to leave home. She always ensured her children had the appropriate clothes for special occasions, but seldom attended. Instead, she remained at home and prepared a feast to celebrate their various milestones.

Petra enjoyed neighbors' visits, although she left the talking to others and mostly cooked for them. Petra listened politely to all the chatter around her, never uttering an unkind word about anyone. She never joined her family and guests at the heavily laden wooden table; she stayed on her feet to serve the meal piping hot, returning to refill the serving bowls or replenish the coffee cups. Always the servant, Petra ate only after everyone else was satisfied.

Petra could never be accused of having idle hands. Even late at night, after the company left and the children were in bed, she often worked by the light of the kerosene lantern on her needlework. Her rough, aging hands deftly added colorful embroidery or tidy rows of crocheting to her dishtowels and pillowcases. Tonight she embroidered a scene for a pillow sham, a black horse and its colt grazing among the grass and wild flowers.

Gust, on the other hand, looked forward to weekends for a break in his workweek. He never drank alone, but he enjoyed the company and the libations of the town tavern on Saturday night. Gust didn't work on the Sabbath except to oversee his children milking the cows and caring for the animals. He faithfully brought his children to church and enjoyed playing the generous host to his Sunday guests. For him, Sundays provided an invigorating change of pace.

Petra realized she had much to be thankful for—a husband who loved her, a nice house, plentiful food, and a healthy family. Nevertheless, she fell into bed bone-tired night after night. Would the work ever end?

Depression and War

The Great Depression took its toll on the Dakotans. Gust and Petra's middle sons, Gilbert and Melvin, met the age requirement in 1936 to work in the federal government's new Civilian Conservation Corps (CCC) camps, established to augment family income. The young men of the CCC built dams and bridges, restored historical structures, developed state parks, and planted millions of trees on the treeless prairie.

Gust decided to enroll his two eligible sons to work in the CCC camps without so much as consulting them. Mel had finished high school, but Gil was pulled out during April of his senior year. Each young man earned forty dollars per month in addition to room, board, and uniforms, in exchange for their manual labor. The government sent thirty-five dollars of that wage home to their parents. With only five dollars spending money, Gil had difficulty coming up with the fee required to take the high school exam at camp. To earn a few dollars, Gil cut hair at camp, a skill he had learned from his uncle. Gil was elated when he wrote the high school exam and earned the diploma that had nearly eluded him. The young brothers ended up in separate camps, not returning home for a visit until Christmas.

At home, that extra seventy dollars a month, every month for three years, made a huge difference to the Shirley family budget. Later, when the youngest son, Glen, became old enough, he also worked in the CCC for six months.

Following his time in the CCC, Mel, the older brother who was short in stature with dark hair, joined the North Dakota National Guard. He rose to the rank of sergeant. When Gil's three-year stint in the CCC ended, the tall, blond athlete was anxious to resume civilian life, but instead he was drafted into the United States Army.

At Camp Claiborne, an officer who recognized Gil from the CCC told him where to find his brother, Mel. The helpful officer "pulled some strings," according to Gil, and assigned him to his brother's tent. After being deployed together on the West Coast guarding vital facilities, in March of 1942, their unit shipped out for duty in the Pacific, arriving in New Caledonia.

Gil and Mel fought together as part of the Army's 164th Infantry Regiment, Americal Division, joining troops of the First Marine Division in the fierce Battle of Guadalcanal, America's first land offensive of the war.

In October of 1942, during a fierce battle, Mel was shot in the shoulder. Gil found his brother, poured sulfa powder into Mel's wound, and alerted medics. But Mel had lost considerable blood and soon lapsed into a coma. Gil was ordered to move on with his unit. With a heavy heart, he realized his brother couldn't survive.

Triage medics evaluated Mel on the battlefield and left him among the mounting pile of dead. Personnel stripped him of his uniform and shoved his dog tags in his teeth for identification.

Meanwhile, Gil's Army unit continued fighting on Guadalcanal for another five months before heading to the Fiji Islands, the Solomon Islands, and finally the Philippine Islands. They teamed with U.S. Marine and Navy personnel in battle, often in hand-to-hand combat. Within months, Gil weighed only 129 pounds, gaunt for his muscular, 5-foot, 11-inch frame. His three cans of meat a day—one with beans, one with corned beef, and one with vegetable stew—plus his daily serving of hardtack biscuit, chocolate bar, and coffee, didn't provide enough calories for the physical demands of the campaign. Later his rations improved with the addition of powdered eggs and lemon drink or cocoa. Gil's closest buddy, Glen Wick, contracted encephalitis. He was lucky to be shipped home to a hospital where he successfully fought for his life.

Back on the Shirley farm, the parents remained in the dark as to the fate of their sons. They had been notified by telegram that Mel was missing, but received no further word. Petra cried often, fearing the worst. Gust, stoic and intensely private, kept working the farm and wouldn't talk about their boys except with Petra. They both prayed for their sons, but months passed with no word, and hope waned. Although they received no news from Gil, they wanted to believe he remained alive somewhere in the vast Pacific war zone. Christmas came and went, a somber holiday that year.

Before their own sons served in the military during wartime, Petra and Gust had witnessed first hand how war destroys lives. Petra's brother, Oscar, had been disabled in World War I and was unable to resume farming. He lived out his life in a veteran's hospital in New York City suffering from shell shock—now called post-traumatic stress disorder and treatable with medication and therapeutic counseling. Gust and Petra feared their own sons might suffer a similar fate, if they survived at all.

Back on the battlefield, Mel regained consciousness as he was about to be removed from Guadalcanal for burial. Fortunately, a Marine medic assigned to the task of transporting the dead from the battlefield spotted Mel's arm twitching. The medic pulled him from the pile of dead bodies, found a pulse, and administered plasma. Mel had apparently spit the dog tags out of his mouth, thereby losing his identity.

The medic diverted the wounded man to a British Marine hospital as an unidentified friendly combatant. Without identification, no one at the hospital knew if Mel was American, British, or an Aussie or his branch of service. When Mel regained consciousness and could finally speak, he proudly identified himself as a U.S. soldier. Mel began a series of stays in various hospitals in the Fiji Islands. He earned the Purple Heart for his injury and the Bronze Star medal for advancing through heavy fire to rescue a wounded officer.

Gust and Petra were still waiting for news in January of 1943. Then one day their eighteen-year-old daughter, Evelyn, received an unexpected letter from a soldier who had returned to the states. The soldier, a stranger to the family, explained in his letter that he had been wounded in Guadalcanal in October, about the same time as Mel, and ended up recovering in the same hospitals in the Fiji Islands. Mel had asked him to write to the Shirley family once the buddy arrived stateside. The letter described Mel's gunshot wound and his remarkable recovery: "He came back quickly when given plasma, and about ten days after he was wounded was up walking. We were fortunate that we had good medical care wherever we went." Mel's buddy concluded with wonderful news, "It will be only a matter of time before he will be in first class shape again."

Evelyn read the letter and let out a squeal. Running to tell her mother, she shouted, "Ma, Ma, Mel is alive. He's wounded, but he's alive." Tears flooded Petra's weathered face as she hugged her daughter. Evelyn then ran to meet her father, Gust, returning from the barn. Elated at the news, they made plans to go to town and share the good news immediately with their little community.

"Evelyn, write and tell the rest of the family about Mel," Gust told his daughter. Although both parents were literate, Petra wrote in Norwegian, not English, and Gust simply didn't write personal letters.

Mel rightfully assumed a letter sent from within the United States would arrive at his home much sooner than one sent from within the war zone. Mail coming or going out of the combat zone was censored, and often delayed from four to six months.

The Shirleys worried for an additional two-and-a-half years about the safety of their other son, Gil, as they followed the daily war reports in the papers and on the radio.

In the spring of 1943, while Gil was fighting in the Fiji Islands, he encountered a military surgeon who had noticed Gil's surname on a roster and sought him out. "Do you know a Melvin Shirley?" the stranger asked. "He's recovering from a gunshot wound in the shoulder."

"That must be my brother! I thought he was dead!" gasped Gil, his heart racing. "Where is he?"

"I'm afraid you just missed him. He left for California just three days ago. But I am his surgeon and can assure you he's going to recover fully."

Indeed, Mel had survived. He'd recovered enough to return for a stateside reassignment. Thankful for the message from this goodhearted stranger, the news gave Gil the needed boost to soldier on. At the conclusion of the war in 1945, the brothers were finally reunited with each other and their family in North Dakota. The proud family felt vastly relieved when both sons returned home able-bodied. They learned how Mel, understanding the hell of war, had prayed daily for his brother's survival.

Gil, promoted to First Sergeant, was honored for his military service and awarded the Bronze Star medal for meritorious service. His unit received a Presidential Citation. "I was one of the lucky ones," said Gil, who survived 628 days of combat, much of it in the jungles of the Pacific.

Experiencing both the unspeakable evils of war and the kindness of strangers, the men's lives remained profoundly changed; they considered each new day of life a gift. Returning to embrace a full family life, each lived to be eighty-seven.

◆   ◆   ◆

Throughout the war, Gust farmed his own homestead and rented the adjoining farmland from his bachelor brother-in-law, Oscar Hanson. Wheat prices held strong during wartime, and that extra acreage provided Gust with added income.

Gust avoided the plight of many of his neighbors who lost their land to taxes. Thousands of farmers, mired in debt, pulled up stakes and left for potential city jobs during the late 1920s and 1930s. Combining his father's original nest egg with hard work, good management, a frugal nature, and a bit of luck, Gust weathered the "dirty thirties" when the drought and blowing dust ended many a dream. Raising six sons to do the farm work certainly helped. An effective organizer, he kept his workers busy. By his forties, Gust managed others instead of doing the heavy work himself.

Gust always lived within his means, refusing to mortgage his land. Often the Shirley family went without services many would consider necessities, such as dental care, rather than borrow money. He proudly declared, "I don't owe anyone a nickel." Remaining debt-free was unusual in the Dakota farming community; heavy indebtedness and foreclosure were common.

Loaves and Fishes

Art Shirley, Evelyn's oldest brother.

"Going to town now to get Jimmy," Gust Shirley told Petra, his white-haired wife.

She nodded while continuing to knead bread in the big mixing bowl. The pungent smell of yeast permeated the kitchen. "It'll be good to have him here," she said.

Nine-year-old Jimmy was their grandson, Hilda's eldest child. He lived in Jamestown, North Dakota, where his father, Andrew Otto, worked in the railroad roundhouse. The young visitor arrived in Robinson by train with a satchel of clothes, ready to spend several weeks during summer vacation.

The year 1943 proved an unusually quiet time on the Shirley farm on the treeless prairie. Gone were the decades when the two-story wooden farmhouse echoed with the voices of children. All of their thirteen children were grown, and all except Art, the eldest, had moved out. No longer did married sons and daughters need to bring home new spouses to stay "until we can find our own place." The unmarried Shirley girls had moved to the city to work, and two sons were serving in the war. Now it was quiet, and Petra, in declining health, spent most of her workday alone with time for an afternoon nap. Lonely and fearful about her sons away at war, she welcomed a child's company.

Other grandchildren visited from time to time, but having Jimmy stay for the summer cheered Petra. Jimmy adored his grandmother and boasted to his classmates that she was the "kindest, best Grandma anywhere."

Petra began preparing her famous Norwegian specialty, *rømmegrøt*. She first collected the cream that had been separated from the whole milk and left to sour. She boiled the unprocessed sour cream in an iron pot, stirring in just enough flour until the butterfat separated. She scooped off the liquid butter and set it aside, added hot milk and a bit more flour to the kettle by sight, not measure. She patiently cooked the sour cream porridge until it thickened, stirring nonstop to keep it from scorching or getting lumpy. Petra served the smooth, white porridge warm with cinnamon and sugar, sometimes ladling melted butter on top. She knew Jimmy loved it.

Red-haired and freckle-faced, Jimmy loved many things about his grandpa's farm: pets, farm animals, and the freedom to roam over acres of open space. He considered helping Art with the milking an adventure, certainly not drudgery. The child seemed to energize Art, a patient man of forty-two, who could be heard singing in a lovely tenor voice as he drove home from the wheat fields.

Jimmy would go fishing on Sunday afternoon, if he could convince Art to drive him a few miles to Lake Williams where perch could be caught from shore. The boy didn't have anything fancy, just a cottonwood pole, sturdy string, and a hook. He dug up worms out of the black, moist soil around the cattle shed. He stored them overnight on the porch in a coffee can covered with a moist rag, so he'd be ready in a moment.

Sometimes he got skunked, but often he caught a couple of fish large enough to eat. Even catching one tiny fish would make Jimmy's day.

Jimmy soon learned from experience that Grandpa would be tired on Sunday after spending a late Saturday night in town drinking with his friends, getting up to attend church, and then downing a big meal. Grandpa needed a Sunday nap, and Jimmy knew he shouldn't disturb him. So Jimmy would pester Art. "Please Art, just for a little while," he'd beg. All he had to do was break down Art's half-hearted resistance, and he'd have a driver and fishing partner.

As a young man, Art had fallen in love with a beautiful, dark-haired hometown girl, Louise. Every Friday afternoon the sandy-haired, good-looking suitor dressed up and drove to pick up Louise from the country school where she taught. They dated for nearly seven years, but he never married her, probably because he couldn't provide for her the way he wanted. He kept expecting he'd get a bumper crop, but the years slipped away. "Louise, my next crop has to be better," he sighed each year.

In the late 1920s and 1930s Gust's house was overcrowded. Art didn't even have the privacy of his own bed or bedroom; he had to share with other extended family members. Art told one of his siblings, "This is certainly no place to bring a new wife." Although he had acquired a quarter section of land and a drinking well, Art had no money to build a house for Louise.

Art had always worked hard at on his father's farm, but tough financial times and a large family to feed prevented Gust from paying Art much salary or lending him money. The homesteading boom that had helped Gust's generation was over. Land was no longer free, and Art and his brothers had a much more difficult time getting established farming

Meanwhile, Louise, a spinster in her late twenties, wanted a family. Perhaps she realized she wasn't getting any younger. One summer day during the Great Depression, a traveling circus came to town where Louise lived with her parents. A few days later, Louise, the love of Art's life, left with a roustabout. The little town buzzed with gossip. Tongues clucked, "Can't believe she'd just up and run away like that."

"Shocking. She'll be back. Just wait and see," speculated others.

But when Louise returned to visit her folks, her new husband accompanied her. The humiliating loss of Louise devastated Art. He fell into a deep depression, rocking in a chair and staring silently out the window for days on end. Petra couldn't console him, and he was unable to work. Gust brought medicine from the doctor, highly unusual when someone was not physically ill.

Art never dated again. He slowly resumed farming and eventually returned to the things he loved to do—hunting, fishing, and singing in a male quartet. In the 1940s, better crops and prices belatedly provided him with a good income, but Louise was gone.

Although Art had long ago accepted his loss of a decade earlier, Jimmy thought his uncle needed a wife. "Art," he suggested one day, "you should marry my fourth-grade teacher, Miss Conway. She's really pretty." But Art only smiled. He didn't tell Jimmy what the adults in the family already knew: If he couldn't have Louise, he'd settle for a bachelor's life.

Soon Jimmy returned to the subject of fishing. Art grumbled, "Gee, Jimmy. I'm tired. Sunday is supposed to be time to rest." But most Sundays he would relent for a short trip to the lake with his nephew.

"We'll bring back enough fish for supper for everyone," Jimmy boasted, grinning as the two drove off towards the lake one hot July afternoon.

With high expectations, Jimmy picked a spot, walked out waist-deep and threw in his fishing line. The dark clouds and sticky air announced a passing summer thunderstorm moving off to the northwest, and the fish rushed at the bait. He soon started pulling in one fish after another almost as fast as he could replace a fat, squirmy worm on the hook.

Art, watching in amazement, never bothered to take out his own pole, but tossed each perch, measuring from six to nine inches each, in a gunny sack lying near the water as the boy caught them. He'd never seen anyone so lucky at fishing. Eventually the fish filled a third of the big sack. Art had trouble convincing the excited, wide-eyed boy that it was time to go home and clean the fish for supper. "C'mon, Jimmy, it's time to go."

"Just one more, Art. Please, just one more," Jimmy begged.

Late in the afternoon Art secured the heavy sack on the running board on the outside of the auto, and they drove back to the farm singing "Down by the Old Mill Stream" over the roar of the motor.

"Grandma, come look. I caught a whole sack of fish!" Jimmy yelled from the porch, displaying his impressive catch.

Petra opened the screen door and chuckled. "Well, guess we'll all have fish for supper after all. Got a lot of fish there to clean. Ask Grandpa and Uncle Olaf if they'll help you."

Art, Gust, and his visiting brother, Olaf, helped Jimmy scale and clean the fish out on the porch, then scrubbed the wooden planks on the porch with soap and water. They buried the inedible parts in the potato patch for fertilizer.

Petra and her sister-in-law and best friend, Hannah, fried up the whole catch of fish in Petra's big iron skillet. The Shirleys sat down to a late supper table laden with the huge platter of fresh fish, along with homemade bread, butter, milk, and coffee. "Pass the fish. Best I ever ate," said Grandpa Gust, patting his ample belly as he winked and licked his fingers.

The proud nine-year-old beamed and couldn't agree more. "Wish my folks and sisters could see how many fish I caught. I can hardly believe it. I'll remember this forever." Then he turned to his favorite uncle, "Hey, Art, let's do this again next Sunday, okay?"

For Jimmy, the sheer number of fish caught that summer afternoon remained a memory to savor. The bond the uncle and nephew forged that summer lasted a lifetime. The two of them hunted and fished whenever Jimmy could visit.

◆   ◆   ◆

Art continued to hunt geese into his nineties. He was nearing his ninety-fifth birthday when he shot his last deer, while hunting alone. Art's vehicle got stuck in the snow about dusk, but he was prepared to spend the freezing night in the car. At dawn, he hiked to the nearest road, sat on an inverted pail he had carried from his vehicle, and waited to be picked up by the first hunter who arrived. After a hot cup of coffee and a hearty breakfast, Art was none the worse for the adventure.

Meanwhile, Gust stayed on his homestead land for over forty years until 1947, when he and Petra retired to a house in Robinson. Art moved along with his folks. Gust's second-oldest son, Orville, took over operation of the family farm for a few years, but had difficulty supporting his own thirteen children in a different era.

Petra looked forward to moving nearer to her best friend, Hannah, who had previously retired to town. Unfortunately, by this time both women suffered frail health and rarely ventured out. After raising thirteen children, giving birth to nine of them, Petra's body simply wore out. Gust cooked for and nursed his bedridden wife, their roles reversed. Petra died at home of complications of coronary artery disease on May 2, 1951, at the age of seventy. Gust buried his beloved Petra in the Shirley plot near their teenage son, Edwin, and Gust's first wife, Othilda, in the church cemetery overlooking his homestead.

In 1960, Gust, age eighty, abruptly sold his land to a neighbor, surprising his family. Individual farms had increased in acreage, so perhaps Gust realized his acreage was no longer sufficient to sustain a family. His middle-aged sons had established careers in other fields; they had no serious interest in farming. Always pragmatic, Gust kept his reasons for selling the land to himself. The land had served his purposes, giving him and his family a good life. He moved on to a new phase, using the proceeds from its sale for his retirement.

Finally free of worry about weather and fluctuating market prices, Gust spent long hours fishing for perch or catfish in the local lakes. He continued using the wooden boat he and his sons had designed and built with the help of a local carpenter.

Gust and Petra Shirley.

Gust Shirley in 1965.

Gust visited with friends daily and savored the smooth taste of whiskey in his golden years. He enjoyed visits from the children and grandchildren who returned to Robinson to see him. A devout Lutheran, he attended church regularly. As the years rolled by, Gust worried that he might outlive his savings. Determined to bequeath a small inheritance to each child, Gust became frugal to a fault. He often turned down the heat in the frigid winter or shut off electricity to save money.

"Pa, why keep it so cold in here?" my mother, Evelyn, would ask when we stopped to visit. "It's too cold for your grandkids to take off their coats and mittens," she said. Dressed in several layers of clothing, Gust would shrug and bring in more coal for the stove.

Fiercely independent, Gust dreaded financially burdening anyone. He disdained accepting charity, although he often helped others in need. He remained reluctant to accept social security checks, because he didn't pay into the system. Fortunately, he fulfilled his wish, able to pay his own way to the end without depleting his savings.

The proud patriarch lived to see thirty-four grandchildren and forty-nine great-grandchildren. He always recognized me, but Gust had difficulty remembering my name; I was known as Evelyn's daughter. Blessed with extraordinary health, Gust lived to age ninety-three, dying May 4, 1972, after a brief illness. He was buried near his wives, in the church cemetery he maintained for decades, forever united with the prairie.

Art lived alone, in good health, for over two decades. Mild-mannered, Art didn't drink or smoke, but never criticized those who did. He had earned the respect of young and old as an amiable elder, sometimes being referred to as the town's favorite son. Never fathering children himself, he became a much-loved uncle to many in the family, as well as in the little farming community, until his death at ninety-six.

Oil!

Oil derrick near Robinson, ND, in 1926. Photo by Carl Wick.

Hard times provided fertile ground for get-rich-quick schemes. On August 24, 1925, a passing motorist drove into the prairie town of Robinson, North Dakota. On that hot summer day he stopped at the town water pump. The visitor retrieved his bucket to get water for his overheated radiator. Instead of water, the stranger pumped out an amber liquid. It tasted and smelled like gasoline. Puzzled, he poured the fluid on a chunk of wood and lit a match. The fluid burst into a cool blue flame. The visitor, now excited, rushed to the local store and demonstrated the phenomenon for a growing crowd of citizens.

"You've got gasoline coming from your well!" the stranger announced, igniting Robinson's hopes of becoming a boomtown.

Locals flocked to the water well situated in the middle of town to see for themselves. The well had been abandoned for several months after it had developed a brackish color. A couple of men anxiously pumped out bucketfuls of what appeared to be refined gasoline.

"Johnny, get some buckets. This here is free gas," one father proclaimed.

"Buckets? Hell, I'm bringing my car," said another.

Soon people were lining up and filling their car gas tanks straight from the well. The need to refine petroleum into gasoline wasn't yet understood by the motoring public who had just converted from horses. The oddity of pumping gas from the well continued for some days until Mr. Nerby, who had title to the well, built a little structure around it complete with a padlock on the door. Any other owner would have done the same.

Limiting access to the free gasoline didn't slow the speculation that the town might be built over a lucrative oil field. After an inspection of individual gasoline tanks ruled out seepage, many shopkeepers were convinced they sat atop an untapped bonanza. They hired geologists who gave conflicting judgments on the source of the gas. One expert told them what they hoped to hear, noting that Calgary, Canada, had experienced similar gas wells that produced highly refined gas. Although a few test wells proved fruitless, bedrock optimism prevailed.

The businessmen organized and incorporated the Robinson Development Company to secure leases for oil-drilling rights from landowners and encourage exploration. My grandfather, Tom Price, was one of those nearby landowners who exchanged the five-year right to drill on his land for much needed cash. For weeks no one spoke of anything but oil. Why couldn't it happen here? What better place for the first producing oil well in North Dakota?

The Roaring Twenties proved disheartening for prairie farmers, with modest yields and poor prices for wheat, their main cash crop. After World War I, farm prices plummeted, putting a substantial number of farms into foreclosure. Many local banks failed. The hard-working generation who had arrived with high hopes watched them slither away with each harvest.

Within days of the discovery at the town pump, Arthur C. Townley, the controversial leader of the Non-Partisan League (NPL) political party, appeared in Robinson. Although he'd never won elected office, he remained one of the most powerful men in North Dakota. The new political party sprung from rural discontent of the marketing practices of the huge grain companies. Townley's platform included state ownership of grain elevators and flour mills, rural credit banks operated at cost, and tax relief for farmers. With the help of the Republicans who controlled the state legislature, Townley got the NPL platform enacted, along with a recall provision used to remove elected officials. The voters recalled several high-ranking office holders, including the governor.

Townley, an ordinary-looking man of forty-five, had a long nose and thinning hair. He had a large, loyal political following and a reputation for passionately fighting for the underdog. People were mesmerized when he spoke. The charismatic orator was the region's most effective organizer.

Townley accompanied another stranger who used a homemade contraption nicknamed a "doodlebug" (deployed only in secret) to locate underground oil reservoirs. Townley and the diviner would walk or drive over the land and wait for the instrument to react. The doodlebug reportedly failed to register positive around the Robinson water well. Taken a couple miles east of town where mineral rights leases were still available, it indicated an underground petroleum field. Surely that was the source of the gasoline.

Townley bought the available leases at the drilling site, and sealed off the property with high fences. He built a bunkhouse for 200 workers and stationed political loyalists to guard the entrance. Twice a week the NPL party faithful brought invited guests, all potential oil investors, to the "Oil Camp" for a revival type meeting.

Tom Price certainly wasn't an NPL man. He embraced the rival Independent Voters Association (IVA), which represented a conservative Republican position. But curiosity inspired him to check out Townley. His daughter later told me that one Sunday afternoon, Tom drove his family to hear the noted orator. The kids grew restless, but Townley impressed the adults as a speaker. Tom noted the huge audience hung on Townley's every word, despite having to stand or sit in the grass in the hot sun. In spite of the optimistic presentation, at the end of the day Tom decided not to invest. My grandmother, Adria, questioned their earlier decision to sell the homestead land's oil rights, but Tom believed in the adage that "a bird in the hand" was more valuable than those running loose.

Meanwhile Townley began raising serious money for oil exploration. He bought a drill rig and began boring through the sandstone. The venture temporarily halted at 150 feet when drillers struck an artesian water stream that flowed under natural pressure. Shortly thereafter, Townley retreated to his Kansas exploration wells for the winter, promising to return. Townspeople considered the flowing water well a good omen. They looked on the delay as temporary. Over the winter they influenced other property owners within two square miles around the drilling site to sell mineral leases to Townley.

The politician-turned-oilman returned the next May as he had promised and resumed drilling with new equipment. A month into the drilling, Townley reported his drill bit was covered with oil. Word leaked out before the *Kidder County Farmers Press* could run a headline declaring "Oil Struck at Robinson." Townley needed still more cash and called a mass meeting. Thousands came.

The day of the big event, the master fundraiser waved a bottle of high-quality crude oil as he intoned, "This came from that oil well, 1200 feet down!" The audience roared its approval. They were looking at evidence with their own eyes. No one knew exactly where he obtained the bottle's contents. The savvy politician didn't quite promise the potential investors a commercially viable well, but declared all signs pointed to that outcome. "This will speak for itself," he declared, appealing to their greed. The tantalizing possibility of paying off their debts, let alone becoming rich, brought cheers from the excited crowds. It was exactly what they wanted to hear.

The *Fargo Forum* newspaper, based one hundred and seventy-five miles away, quoted Townley at the rally. Somehow it sounded more convincing when Townley declared it in person than when it was quoted in the paper. "Loan me your money, but kiss it goodbye. There may be oil here. I am convinced that there is, but there may not. If we strike oil it will make us all rich, there will be plenty of money to pay off mortgages, and all other debts, and then some. The money is to be used to drill for oil in both North Dakota and Kansas, or elsewhere."

More drilling required more money. Townley reminded investors that to bring the oil to market he'd be obliged to drill much deeper to reach the source. After his rousing speech, the crowds clamored to invest $100 to $500, often relinquishing savings that had been earmarked for taxes or seed for planting. Public disclosure laws didn't exist, but it is believed Townley collected up to a half million dollars, an unbelievable amount in 1926. Becoming increasingly skeptical, Tom still declined to invest. "You'll be sorry, Tom," a friend chided him.

"Don't think so. Seems too good to be true."

With great anticipation the drilling resumed, although all activities remained secret as before. People drove up to the gate hoping for a peek at prosperity. "Find anything yet?" They were turned away with the promise they'd be notified as soon as Townley struck oil.

Weeks turned into months. No news eventually became bad news. Ultimately the oil well was declared dry, and the camp was dismantled without fanfare. The dream of sudden prosperity burst. All the money was gone; the investors had no recourse. Townley's drilling efforts in Kansas also ended in failure.

Despair set in. For some farmers who now couldn't repay their operating loans, it became the final straw. Angry and embarrassed, many pulled up stakes and moved, abandoning debts throughout the community. Their homesteading ventures ended in failure, hastened by a belief in snake oil.

Busted in California

In the late spring of 1929, Tom and Adria Price decided to return to California to live. They rented out their farmland and sold some of their farm equipment and cattle. They packed up and drove west once more. Tom planned to repair shoes, a skill not so different than that of repairing leather harnesses, which he did so well.

Their timing in moving from the farm to the city was terrible. The Great Depression had created havoc across America. Tom soon wondered if his family would have been better off on his North Dakota farm, where they could grow their own food.

Tom's Hawthorne, California, shoe repair shop.

Business at his shoe repair shop in Hawthorne, CA, was struggling. Tom came home from work one day particularly discouraged. "George White came by today and told me he lost his job," Tom told his wife.

Adria was saddened. "Poor man. Resorting to bread lines will be painful."

"He has no choice with four youngsters to feed. George has been a loyal customer. He couldn't pay me for fixing his boots, but I gave them back to him anyway. I knew he'd pay me if he could."

"That was the right thing to do, Tom."

"Yeah, George might as well wear them. Nobody's likely to buy them, even for the cost of repairs. No one has money. Wonder how long I can go on with no paying customers. Maybe we should move back."

"I don't know. I just got a letter from my brother, Edward, and it sounds pretty bad in Dakota, too," Adria said. "Listen to what he writes. 'Times are worse now than anything we have ever known as to money. People seem to have plenty to eat and wear thus far, but before winter is over the county charity lines will be long.'"

Adria looked up. "How sad. Here's what Edward says about prices. 'Just think of selling wheat for thirty cents per bushel and rye for twenty cents. I sold one sow weighing 515 pounds for thirteen dollars. Banks do not loan any money. People do not pay old bills and get all the credit they can. Everything is at a standstill.'"

In his letter Edward recommended that Tom begin foreclosure on his tenant farmer who had not paid rent or taxes as contracted. Tom risked losing his land. Despite gnawing uneasiness, Tom gave his tenant, Mr. B——, one last chance and reluctantly signed a revised contract for another growing season. He extended Mr. B—— new terms to buy the land or pay delinquent rent and taxes before November of 1932. Tom thought surely the crops and prices would improve and he'd get paid. But Mr. B—— became further disillusioned with farming and didn't even finish planting crops. He survived on income from his second job as a railroad depot agent while he and his family lived on Tom's farm without paying rent.

While still living in California, Tom and Adria heard about the Robinson fire. The twenty-year-old village of Robinson had been struggling, boom times already a fond memory. In January 1932, the dread word—*Fire!*—rang out. A fire swept through a row of wooden frame buildings on Main Street, burning them to the ground. There was no equipment to slow the fire's advance, and soon only the brick bank building remained standing on the west side of the block. The flash fire had started in the living quarters of the post office, destroying that building along with the two general stores.

Thankfully, no one was hurt. Swanson's Store relocated, but the proprietor of Waxman's Store moved on. The post office moved into the rear of the bank.

Finally, in September of 1932, the Prices were forced to return to North Dakota and legally evict their renter. After three years of broken promises and no income from the farmland, they faced the looming threat of losing Tom's homestead to the county for back taxes.

Tom sold his shoe repair shop and shipped the family furniture by rail. He hoped to keep both California houses rented, as real estate prices were too low to sell. He didn't know just when the family might return. Until that time, he could only hope that rent would cover taxes, fire insurance, and the ever-increasing street assessments.

Eight-year-old Bruce gave up his coveted spot selling the *Los Angeles Times* at the local market. He dutifully let his mother deposit his last earnings in his bank account for safekeeping. He and his older sister, Pearl, said goodbye to their friends and helped find a home for their pet dog, Buster. Then Bruce made one last trip to the local feed store to bid farewell to his special friend, the owner's pet monkey.

Adria dreaded going back to the isolation of the farm and its primitive farmhouse. She had grown accustomed to the conveniences of indoor plumbing, gas heat, and electricity, none of which existed on the farm. She couldn't hold back the tears as they packed their belongings into a homemade trailer hitched to their green 1928 Chevy.

Providing schooling for her children remained Adria's top priority. In California her task was simple, because the family lived right across from Washington Street School. She tried to explain the situation to her California neighbor. "Here I watch them cross the street and enter the schoolyard on their own. Back in Dakota, Tom will have to drive them by auto the five-and-a-half miles when roads are good. In winter Tom must either take them by horse and sleigh to town, or I must stay with them in a rental house near the school."

Pearl later told me her mother sobbed when Adria bid farewell to her neighbors and friends at church. "I'm going to miss the Inglewood Library, too, just a short streetcar ride away," she told them.

With a wave and a promise to write, the Price family began their 1500-mile odyssey during a September heat wave. They couldn't have known they would never return. They drove north on the Ridge Route over the Tejon Pass and down the Grapevine, climbing out of the Los Angeles basin and heading north through the San Joaquin Valley. The old touring car groaned under the weight of the trailer loaded with clothes, dishes, and household items. The radiator repeatedly overheated as they ascended the mountain pass.

Adria became carsick and sweated so much she worried about the money orders stashed in her corset. "What if the ink smears?" she wondered. At one radiator stop they filled Adria's scrub bucket with cold water so she could soak her feet while she rode. Unfortunately, the muffler under the thin auto floorboards quickly heated up the water. "Ouch, it's getting hot! This isn't working."

That first night the family pitched their canvas tent and ate sandwiches. Adria laid out the damp, but still legible, financial documents on the tent floor to dry.

The family continued northbound and stopped to see Tom's brother, Frances (Frank) in Oroville, California, but couldn't stay long. Tom needed to cross the Rocky Mountains before snow closed the passes. He hoped to make better time this trip, because more gravel roads had been built across the country. Pavement remained a rarity in 1932.

Once they left California's long central valley and headed east, temperatures moderated. One night a strong storm with driving rain collapsed their tent as they slept. "Everyone alright?" Tom asked, while untangling the canvas tent and attempting to temporarily prop it back up. "Yeah," Pearl said, struggling towards the center of the tent. "But I'm getting wet!"

Closer inspection revealed one side of the tent had ripped. Tom secured it as best he could and waited for the storm to pass. The howling winds kept them awake as they huddled together. In the daylight they surveyed the damage. "We'd better find a hotel tonight." Tom said. "I could repair the tent, but I don't have enough tools with me. Damn it. Hadn't planned to spend money on hotels."

While packing up their damp possessions, Pearl discovered her favorite blue dress was missing. "Ma, it's gone. I know I folded it up and put it right next to me last night." She and Bruce searched the area with no luck. "Come on, Pearl, we must go. The wind blew it away. It's lost," said her mother. Pearl reluctantly climbed into the car.

After the nighttime downpour, the travelers faced a new road hazard—mud. The dirt roads turned to muddy ruts, and the car mired down. At times the family had to get out and push the Chevy through the slimy sludge. "This is hard work," Pearl whined. "My shoes are getting all muddy."

"Quit complaining. At least we haven't had to push uphill," Tom said. "Adria, do you remember how we once had to back the old Model T Ford up that steep incline in Idaho?"

"How could I forget?"

Several days later, the weary Prices arrived back in Steele, North Dakota, trying to adjust to the climate change. The brisk, clear autumn days became nights with near-freezing temperatures.

Tom and Adria evicted the tenant, moved onto the farmstead, and set about putting their property back in order.

The children rejoined their old classmates. Soon winter arrived. The rural roads were blocked with snow most of the winter, so Adria and the children rented a small house in Robinson, closer to school. Tom remained on the farm to tend the livestock, joining the family when weather permitted travel.

Again, they believed things would improve in the spring. As before, Tom was drawn back to his land, this time so he could grow food to feed his family. He still had faith in the land. Each time a door closed, Tom returned to the land.

Spring came. They planted, but the rains didn't return. The hot winds of summer quickly burnt the emerging wheat and oat crops once again. Farmers worried about having cattle feed through the grazing season as the grass in the pastures shriveled up and thistles took over. Tom gazed over the brown pastures and worried that his livestock might starve. He scanned the sky for signs of rain. How long could this drought go on?

A Season of Sorrow: Drought, Death, and Taxes

After their 1932 return to North Dakota, the Prices tried to survive without income. Tom traded their two Hawthorne, California, houses to his brother-in-law, Ed Williams, for more Dakota farmland. Their savings nearly depleted, they mortgaged Tom's homestead farm, after finally evicting the defaulting buyer.

Tom still believed raising cattle was his best chance to earn a profit, even if his wheat crop failed. The next year he moved his family once again, this time to the second farmstead, the Checkerboard Farm, because of its bigger barn. Never mind that the tiny house had fallen into disrepair—they'd make do. By now the bold red-and-white checkerboard pattern on the barn doors had faded, but paint and improvements must wait until better days. Tom reluctantly borrowed money from the government to buy feed grains for his livestock. He prayed the cattle would ultimately provide him desperately needed income. Besides raising their meat, they produced a small garden, eggs, and dairy products. At sixty-three, Tom wasn't about to give up and resort to charity. They never missed a meal, as they feared might happen in the city.

Tom and Adria had a long-running quarrel, not about the serious issues of money and housing, but about her hair. Rather old-fashioned, Tom showed displeasure when his wife returned from town sporting a modern above-the-shoulders bobbed haircut. Adria loved the up-to-date style, relieved it would require less care than her long, unruly hair.

"But a woman's hair is her crowning glory. Why would you cut it off?" Tom asked.

"I didn't cut it off, it's just shorter. It'll be easier to care for," she answered. "I like it!"

"Well, I don't!"

Bruce periodically received an interest check for ten cents on his California savings account. When he presented the first check at the local bank, he learned it cost a dime to cash an out-of-area check. Soon the checks stopped coming. The bank had failed, swallowing up his money and that of his family. He no doubt wished he'd spent his newspaper earnings on candy.

Meanwhile, political agitation increased all around them. Largely because of economics, the state experienced turbulent political times. Tom and Adria followed news and politics closely, gathering around the noisy, static-filled radio. They subscribed to a daily paper, their window to the outside world, delivered to Robinson by train from Fargo. They gave up many other amenities before they canceled their paper.

When the roads remained passable, the rural mail carriers gathered up the mail and newspapers from the post office and delivered them to the farms three times a week. Farmers collected their newspapers and parcels on each trip to town. One day John Wilkins hailed Tom as he approached the Price farm on horseback. "Hey, dropping off your mail, Tom. You've got newspapers to catch up on, a package from Sears, and a letter from your brother."

"Thanks John. Appreciate it. Can you stop for coffee?"

"No, thanks. Not today. Got to get back before dark. Tell Adria that the Nelsons had a baby boy. See you at the primary election."

Tom often debated politics with the neighbors, especially those supporting the Non-Partisan League. "See what a damn fix we're in. Old Bill Langer [North Dakota's indicted governor] is a crook!" declared Tom. Feelings ran strong among all those facing abject poverty.

Adria and Tom never missed voting. Both registered as Republican, but would vote for a Democrat if they thought their party's candidate lacked integrity. Adria had staunchly supported Herbert Hoover since 1928, based on her personal knowledge of his competence when Hoover was running the U.S. Food Administration during the Great War. She'd been appointed to a county leadership post within that organization and remained loyal to her former boss, even in the midst of the Great Depression. Tom, on the other hand, was fed up with Hoover, especially after he read about an alleged Red Cross scandal.

In 1932 he voted Democrat, for Roosevelt. The couple argued heatedly about politicians. "You're just going to cancel out my vote," Tom complained that election day. But he didn't dare leave his wife at home when he went to the polls. She prized the newly won right to vote and intended to exercise it at every opportunity. Tom eventually became an independent.

Scores of families had failed to make a profit and had already left the prairies in the 1920s and early '30s, including those counting on the oil bonanza that never materialized. Some of their former neighbors took an opposite journey from Tom and Adria, leaving the farm and heading west toward the coastal cities, hoping for factory employment or at least a public works job.

Adria considered going back to teaching, but realized she no longer had the physical stamina. She also knew heads of household received preferential hiring. The county needed fewer teachers now with declining enrollment, and the teachers working didn't always get paid. Not only had the overall population declined, but also in hard times fewer students remained in school past the mandatory eighth grade. Instead of attending high school, they left the farm to find employment.

Throughout the country, young, able-bodied men were hired for federal government construction crews to build sidewalks, town halls, post offices, bridges, soil erosion projects, or plant trees. Tom was too old, and Bruce too young. So the boy, a ninth grader, and Pearl, a sixteen-year-old high school senior, helped at home and attended school. They talked of continuing beyond high school. "I hope we can send you both to college," said Adria. But Tom harbored serious doubts and became despondent about the economic realities.

Pearl decided to follow in her mother's footsteps and become a teacher, provided they could borrow tuition for teacher's training. Bruce, unsure about his future, began dreaming of the various trade courses, such as printing or mechanics, offered at his mother's alma mater.

By 1935, Adria began experiencing serious health problems. She suffered from apparent high blood pressure and kept experiencing severe nosebleeds that left her weak. Sometimes Tom stopped the nosebleeds by applying snow to her head.

Old Doc Baer from Steele noted her declining health, but didn't know how to help her. No train ran between Robinson and Steele, only poorly graded roads, so keeping doctor's appointments proved difficult. Dr. Baer suggested Adria might be better off in Steele near him, but that was expensive and impractical.

"I need to be near my family," she told him. "They're attending school in Robinson. This winter I can take the train from Robinson to Woodworth [a town to the east] to see Dr. Melzer, if I must."

Mrs. Mary Bon, her neighbor and confidant, later summed it up over a cup of tea. "Well, let's all pray for a short, mild winter. Adria, you worry me. You don't look so well. You're moving slow, and you're losing weight."

"Oh, I'll be alright. Medicine will keep me going until spring."

The winter of 1935–36 proved anything but mild. The state posted the coldest stretch of weather ever recorded for the forty-eight contiguous states. At one official weather station in North Dakota, the temperature remained below freezing for ninety-six days. The area recorded the biggest snowfall in ten years. Heavy snow banks blocked the roads, rendering autos useless. Even the trains, the lifeline of the prairie town, carrying mail, passengers, and freight, stalled for days due to huge snowdrifts covering the tracks.

In early winter, Adria summoned the strength to make a train trip to see Dr. Melzer who gave her medication. A few weeks later Tom rode into Robinson to use the town's one telephone to contact the doctor again.

"Cold enough for you?" asked Mrs. Bullis, who served as telephone operator inside the Bullis Hotel. Tom nodded as he stamped the loose snow from his overshoes at the doormat.

"How's Adria doing?"

"Not so good, ma'am. Need to call Dr. Melzer."

"I'll put you right through."

Tom spoke with the physician describing his wife's condition. The doctor prescribed additional hypertension medicine and promised to send it to her on the next westbound train. Neither man suggested hospitalization.

The next day, fourteen-year-old Bruce rode his horse into Robinson. He expected to meet the train and retrieve the potentially life-saving medicine for his mother. But the weather had deteriorated and snowdrifts blocked the rails. The train didn't arrive.

Each morning for the next several days, the Prices woke up to temperatures of twenty to forty degrees below zero. Bruce made the grueling eleven-mile horseback trip while Tom cared for his livestock and helped Pearl nurse Adria, now bedridden. The family kept watch for the lone rider to appear on the horizon.

"Did it come?" Tom asked as he made his way to the horse barn to meet his son.

Bruce shook his head, on the verge of tears. The frigid temperatures steadily took their toll on the horse and its young rider, as each night Bruce returned home empty-handed and heartbroken.

"Damn, what are we going to do? We can't move her in this cold. She got worse again today."

By the time the medicine finally arrived, Adria was gravely ill. She showed slight improvement when Bruce and Pearl returned to school after Christmas, boarding in town. But her strength didn't last. One frigid day, Tom summoned a passing neighbor to bring the children back home and call for a doctor.

The neighbor transported Pearl and Bruce back to the farm bundled in a horse-drawn sleigh. However, they were unable to get the distant doctor to the farm. Both Tom and Adria knew the end was near.

Adria's untimely death at age fifty-four came Tuesday, February 11, 1936, with her husband and children at her side.

The neighbors, accustomed to taking care of their own, rallied round to support the family. "We're here to help," they assured Tom. And help they did. Death was all too commonplace in their midst.

The neighbors brought food. They were unable to get the body to an undertaker, so Mrs. Bon washed and dressed the lifeless Adria and fixed her hair. She then laid out her friend in the frigid enclosed porch of the family farm home, awaiting a coffin. Bruce was admonished to watch over her.

All the while they applauded Bruce for "taking it like a man" and not showing much emotion in public. His insides felt ripped open, but he knew he wasn't supposed to cry.

Forlorn February Funeral

Tom made it into town on horseback in the forty below zero temperatures to make funeral arrangements. The widower, numb with cold and grief, sent telegrams notifying Adria's parents and brothers. He scheduled the funeral for that Saturday, February 15, 1936, hoping for a break in the weather. He ordered a coffin costing $100, on account, from Swanson's Store to be delivered to Robinson by train. Next, Tom chose a new wool suit for the funeral.

Carl Swanson, the storekeeper, spoke gently. "This dark one would be a good choice, Tom. It fits you well and will be quite serviceable. It's twenty-five dollars." Tom nodded.

"I'll add it to your tab."

Neither of them could have known Tom would have little opportunity to wear his last suit.

Meanwhile, neighbor men took turns chipping out a grave from the frozen earth using dynamite sticks, axes, and picks. The temperature continued to hover around forty to forty-five degrees below zero. Even with sheepskin coats, overshoes, fur-lined gloves, and wool scarves wrapped over their faces, they could only labor a short time in the brutal cold before risking frostbite. Every deep breath of frigid air caused agonizing pain as they toiled in the wind-swept cemetery. They had to breathe shallowly, more like sniffing, to avoid a painful stab at each inhale. The mucus in their nostrils stung and turned slushy. They squeezed their eyes shut to keep them from icing up and tried to keep their mouths closed, covering them with scarves. The men became aware of their own skeletons as their joints and bones ached in the biting cold. The gravediggers alternated digging in half-hour shifts and then taking shelter at the nearby home of Gust Shirley. There they fortified themselves with hot soup and black coffee and tried to warm their extremities.

Most of Adria's family lived in other states, but by Saturday two of her brothers, Clarence and Edward, arrived by train. Her father, John, couldn't travel, but Mary Williams braved the frigid cold and made the journey from Fargo by train to help bury her only daughter.

"Our condolences, ma'am. We all respected Mrs. Price. It's a terrible loss. Nothing anyone could do," said the Robinson agent as he helped Mrs. Williams down the icy steps at the train depot to the waiting family.

"I've always been proud of her," said Mrs. Williams.

"Yes, ma'am."

The agent moved on to the next car and unloaded a pine casket.

When Saturday dawned the thermometer registered an astounding fifty-one degrees Fahrenheit below zero. At this low ebb in the life of the Price family, an official weather-reporting station in Parshall, North Dakota, registered minus sixty degrees, the lowest reading in the state's recorded history, without considering the wind-chill factor.

Despite the lack of home phones, word-of-mouth quickly spread news of Adria's death and funeral. On Saturday the locals arrived by horse and sled from all directions. The newspaper report later commented on the large numbers attending the funeral in spite of the dangerously cold weather. Neighbors had come to pay their respects to Adria. Highly regarded, she had maintained her unsullied reputation to the end.

A lonely horse and wooden sled transported Adria's coffin from the farm to the Methodist church for services, then on to the Robinson cemetery. A handful of men lowered it into the frozen earth.

Most mourners stayed behind at the clapboard church basement where the ladies served hearty casseroles and homemade cake. Throughout the week Tom had remained dry-eyed and stoic. Bruce and Pearl looked uncomfortable at the reception, no doubt aware they were the center of attention. Bruce couldn't eat, and no doubt wished the well-meaning people would just go away.

A neighbor lady spoke with Adria's mother. "Mrs. Williams, do you think Dr. Baer could've saved her?"

"Perhaps, but Doc didn't even know why she was ill. He told me last fall he didn't think she'd last the winter. Maybe things would've been different if she'd been close by him in Steele instead of being isolated out on that farm."

Later at home with just the kinfolk present, Adria's brother, Clarence, said gently to Tom, "I know it's going to be hard."

Tom's tears finally came, in torrents. "I wish I'd known how sick she was. No one told me. Maybe if she'd stayed in town ..."

"I think she wanted to stay near you and the children," Clarence responded.

Pearl and Bruce had never seen their father cry. Now they dared express their own anguish.

Adria was the only one in her birth family to die before their eighth or ninth decade, except for one infant brother. Although weather and road conditions prevented her from getting medical care in her final days, the relatives could only speculate whether any doctor could have saved her with the medicines then available. Her illness remained undiagnosed. Dr. Baer listed "cause unknown" on her official death certificate.

The decade of the 1930s truly proved a time of broken dreams. Tom struggled on, devastated by his personal loss. He planned to enlarge his herd of coveted Aberdeen Angus beef cattle, and sometimes bartered his livestock for goods and services within the community. The market value of his animals often didn't add up to the cost of their feed. He constantly borrowed on account and juggled overdue bills, but continued to pay for the children's board near school. He was heard muttering, "Always borrowing from Peter to pay Paul."

Tom also had to choose between paying land taxes or maintaining fire insurance on his buildings. Perhaps land could be redeemed later if he lost it to the county over taxes. He knew firsthand the permanence of fire loss.

When spring, the season of hope, finally came, Tom planted again. Pearl graduated from high school that May at age sixteen. She was thrilled when her grandmother Mary came by train for the ceremony. Without funds to attend college, Pearl remained at home, keeping house for her father and brother. The summer seemed unending for the Prices while they tried to adjust to the void in their lives. Working from early morning to dusk gave them a routine, but didn't dull the pain.

The spring temperatures quickly escalated into unmerciful summer heat. The same year that North Dakota plunged to its all-time low temperature, it recorded its highest reading at Steele, 121 degrees Fahrenheit on July 6, 1936. The rains did not come, only dust storms and insects. Dirt stung nostrils and eyes, and static electricity filled the air. Once again Tom's grain crops shriveled and died. "When will it rain?" he agonized.

Desperately trying to retain his sense of humor, Tom baited Harry, his neighbor. "Say, Harry, I heard some commotion outside in my yard during the night. Heard the dog barking and pigs squealing. Then I saw a strange Ford truck backed up next to my pig pen."

Harry bit. "Really? Someone stealing your pigs?"

"No, not stealing them, dropping them off! Now I've got to pay to feed 'em." The farmers roared with laughter at the irony of their plight.

Meanwhile Pearl learned the county had set up a program for seamstresses, seventeen and older, to be paid at a piecework rate. She recognized the unique opportunity for young, single women. No doubt it looked more appealing than keeping house on the farm indefinitely. Pearl spoke privately to her father, noting, "I could earn money by sewing. I know I could do it. But I'm not seventeen yet. Think I should lie about my age?"

Tom silently puffed on his pipe and then responded, "You don't have to lie. Your real birthday is September 12th. You're already seventeen, so go ahead and apply for the job tomorrow." He then abruptly left.

Pearl, stunned by the revelation, knew he spoke the truth. She also knew better than to bring up the birthday discrepancy with him again. Embarrassed by what this implied, she continued to celebrate her February birthday as she always had. She didn't tell her closest girlfriends or her younger brother, perpetuating the deception in their home where honesty had been demanded in all other matters.

Showing leadership skills, Pearl ended up supervising the Robinson seamstress program. The young ladies brought their sewing machines to a vacant room in the schoolhouse and sewed baby layettes and blankets to distribute to the county's poorest.

Pearl next secured a $150 government loan for tuition that allowed her to attend a teacher's training course in Valley City. She passed the qualifying exam and earned her one-year teaching credential. Quickly hired as a teacher in a rural Robinson school, she became a wage earner, getting fifty dollars a month, minus sixteen dollars for board. Tom was pleased. He knew Adria would have been proud.

The Great Depression and Politics

In 1935, construction of a rock and mortar community hall sparked optimism in the struggling town. They built the impressive building, a Works Project Administration (WPA) project, on Main Street on the fire-ravaged lots.

Each time Tom visited Robinson, he surveyed the progress of the new hall with his buddy, Pete Konningrud, the construction foreman. "That stone wall looks pretty straight, Pete. Now be sure to get those doors square," Tom said with a grin. "And make them tall enough so I don't have to duck." Pete chuckled at the good-natured ribbing. Although generally dubious of government intervention, Tom recognized the positive impact the WPA projects had in his town, putting willing people back to work.

Robinson scheduled the grand dedication of the hall for September, 1937. The celebration provided a welcome diversion, a highlight in an otherwise hot, dirty, and depressing decade for the community. Local citizens celebrated in style with band concerts and patriotic singing, a softball game with neighboring Dawson, street races, and a dance with Tom Guttenberg's Radio Orchestra. There were also addresses by a WPA official and their United States Senator, Gerald P. Nye. Senator Nye wore a white summer suit with a blue dress shirt to address the huge crowd. Although his views on fashion were cutting-edge, his isolationist beliefs sounded dated after the Great War. He spoke eloquently about staying out of Europe's affairs, emphasizing that America had enough problems of its own, but his listeners seemed divided on the issue.

The new "town hall," as everybody called it, served as the site of elections, basketball games, graduations, and dances over the years. A private electrical power-plant generator originally provided light for the building, as rural electrification was still a dream. A tractor ran the generator providing power for lights. Sometimes the tractor motor would stall or run out of fuel in the middle of an event. The waiting crowd chanted "Ole, Ole" to summon the town's electrician to restart his tractor and bring back the lights so the game or dance could resume. Ole, often located at the bar playing cards, usually restored lights within ten minutes of being dispatched. In the meantime, cigarette lighters appeared throughout the darkened hall. Although property theft was rare, a few opportunists took advantage of the dark to steal a kiss from their favorite girl.

Thirteen-year-old Evelyn Shirley, Gust's youngest daughter, attended her first dance the night of the dedication. She confided to her mother that she felt special in her Sears and Roebuck rose-colored dress. It featured a sixteen-gore skirt that twirled when she waltzed. "I had one of the prettiest dresses there," she exclaimed the next morning. Bruce Price, too shy to dance, had spotted the pretty, petite blonde and noticed she'd grown up. "I wonder where she learned to dance?" he asked a friend.

Bruce remained a slender, short boy into high school. "Oh, just wait, you'll be as big and tall as your dad," the neighbors had often said.

"Yeah, right," he said, "I'm still no taller than my silly sister. That's not fair."

From childhood, Bruce had idolized his father. He inherited his facial features, but not his father's tall, wide-shouldered physique. Although strong for his slender build, Bruce didn't excel as a boxer or ever "look like a sheriff."

Finally Bruce experienced a growth spurt. Within a few months he grew nine inches to his adult height of five feet, ten inches. For a time, the rapid growth weakened him. Doc thought he heard a heart murmur and prescribed rest, even restricting participation in his physical education classes at school. Bruce's condition meant Tom temporarily lost his only helper on the farm. By Tom's sixty-ninth birthday the physical workload had taken its toll, but he couldn't quit or afford hired help. It was Tom working alone, one man against the elements.

One year merged into another as the Great Depression ravaged the economy. Clouds of buzzing grasshoppers arrived and devoured anything growing. In desperation, farmers spread poison made of arsenic and bran and killed millions of the insects. Still they kept coming. Tom hung on to the land with government feed and seed loans along with personal loans and bank mortgages.

Meanwhile, Tom soured on politics. No rain, depressed farm prices, and desperate economics had spawned radical politicians. Voters throughout North Dakota grew volatile. Four separate men held the governor's office in quick succession due to death, then conviction, and finally recall. "Hate to turn on the damn radio and listen to those idiots," Tom lamented.

If the regional political news was depressing, the world news of fighting in Europe began sounding ominous. Tom dreaded the prospect of another war and worried about another conscription. Bruce had nearly finished high school and could be a prime candidate. Tom felt grateful that he'd lived to see his son reach manhood.

Tom couldn't afford to travel, but kept in touch with his siblings by mail. He read his brother's 1938 Christmas letter, telling of George's financial struggles and distaste for those giving up and going on relief. The letter read, "Sure spoils them for they think the Gov. will keep them, and us poor suckers that are paying taxes and working our heads off are paying for it [relief]."

Tom shuddered. He'd avoided relief thus far, but his brother had no idea that Tom had fallen behind on land taxes. Tom's pride prevented him from sharing this. He suddenly felt alone. Adria would have understood their plight. If only she had lived.

"It's tough everywhere," Tom told his friend, Arnie. "But I'm still better off on the land." He gazed out across his snow-covered acres, acknowledging his near obsession with land. "At least nobody's taken it away. If I get a crop for the next year or two, I'll pay off those damn taxes. That's all I need, a couple good years."

Tom loved horses.

Tom at the wheel of the new invention.

A Life's Work

Tom Price's love of horses was well known throughout the region. He'd spent most of his life training them to the saddle or harness, working with them, nurturing them. Keeping horses or cattle wasn't easy in North Dakota's climate, especially on this bone-chilling February morning, 1939. But Tom worried about his animals. They depended on him.

Tom hauled his six-foot frame out of his warm bed and restarted the fire in the coal stove. He bundled up in his sheepskin coat and hat, and trudged through the snow to the barn, checking first on the animal's water supply. The water in their tank had frozen solid. With several quick strokes of his axe, the aging farmer broke through the ice covering and gave his livestock access to its water. Next he pitched hay to feed his small herd of beef cattle and his eight horses.

Becoming aware of his aching arm, Tom felt strangely dizzy. *Why am I so tired?* he thought. *Just got up. Must be getting old. Well, almost finished. I'll just bring the horses some ground oats before going back to the house to warm up.*

"You're lucky I've got oats left, considering this damn Depression," he told his horses as he entered their corral. Tom gazed with pride at the spirited black gelding who anxiously awaited his morning treat. Then suddenly everything went blurry. Panic and confusion set in. *Something's wrong. Gotta get back to the house.*

He slowly backtracked to the house through the path in the snow. Tom fumbled with the doorknob and managed to open the front door. He dragged himself inside, and then leaned his weakened body against the door, closing it against the icy wind. He felt the welcome blast of heat coming from the coal heater he'd fired up before going to the barn.

127

Just a few more steps to the bed, Tom thought. He backed up against the door and pulled his heavy hat and gloves off one at a time, letting them fall to the floor. *I'll just warm these fingers before lying down,* he thought as he shuffled forward. He stretched out his aching hands towards the beckoning heat of the stove. Then he lost his balance and everything went black.

Several hours passed before John Wilkins, a neighbor living a mile to the east, noticed something odd. Tom's front barn door had remained wide open throughout the frigid day. Normally the door would only be opened briefly in the morning and evening, during chore time. John decided to investigate.

He drove his horse and buggy up to the barn and called out through the open door, but heard no response. John secured his horse and trudged through the snow to the barn looking for Tom. The water tank had been chopped open. He found cattle and horses with remnants of hay left in their feeder, but no Tom. John left the barn, closed its door against the elements, and made his way to the house. He banged on the door. Again no response. John opened the door and noticed the house was cold. He stepped inside. "Tom! My God, what happened?"

Tom remained motionless, slumped against the coal stove with his hands outstretched in front of him. John rushed over to examine him, pulling him to the nearby chair. He noticed with horror that the palms of Tom's hands were burned, although the fire felt stone cold. He found a pulse and detected shallow breathing. His friend was still alive, but in bad shape. The outdoor temperature hovered well below zero, so John knew it hadn't taken long for the fire to burn itself out.

"Can you hear me, Tom? I'm going to get you to some help," said John, talking as much to himself as to Tom, who registered no response. "Sure wish we had phones. Maybe you could've called me for help. Lord knows we're on our own if we get into trouble."

John couldn't afford the time to ride to another neighbor's farm for assistance, so he moved the buggy as close to the house as possible and, with adrenaline pumping, struggled to load Tom's unconscious body. John covered his old friend with sheepskins for the cold seventeen-mile journey to the doctor, stopping enroute to tell another neighbor to care for Tom's animals that evening and try to get word to Bruce and Pearl. Bruce was boarding in Robinson to attend high school, while Pearl was teaching in a one-room school about ten miles away.

Once they arrived in Steele, Doc Baer shook his head sadly and admitted he probably couldn't save the patient. "It's a stroke. He's pretty far gone. We'll just have to wait and see."

The doctor bandaged Tom's burned hands and admitted him to the small hospital. He asked the young kitchen maid to keep vigil throughout the night in case the patient regained consciousness.

Pearl and Bruce arrived in Steele, but Doc Baer, intending to spare the children, refused to let them see their dying father although they begged to say goodbye. Meanwhile, Tom hung on for nearly three days without regaining consciousness before he slipped away.

Once again neighbors chipped a grave into the frozen earth.

As if trapped in a recurring nightmare, Pearl and Bruce once again went through the raw agony of losing a parent, almost three years to the day after Adria's passing. They endured another public funeral and meal at the church, this time with two of Tom's out-of-state brothers in attendance. As Bruce listened to the quartet singing hymns, he fought back tears. Somehow he felt responsible. *Maybe I could have prevented this tragedy.* He kicked himself for not coming home the prior weekend. *If only I'd been there to help.* Pearl was numb. She couldn't believe her parents were both gone.

Tom's obituary summed up the feelings of the community: "Mr. Price was a good citizen and had a legion of friends thru out [*sic*] the county who will regret to hear of his demise."

◆   ◆   ◆

March, 1939. A full month had passed.

"Hello Harry, cold enough for you?" John Wilkins called out as a neighbor arrived on horseback at Tom Price's farmstead.

"When's spring gonna get here? Most of the snow thawed last week. I'm sick and tired of the cold. Hope this is the end of it," replied Harry.

"Wouldn't count on it," said John, speaking slowly. "Ed's already here. He's got the kitchen stove going. Making some coffee. Put your horse away with the others and join us. Bruce told us to make ourselves at home until he could get here from town."

The men had come to take a court-ordered inventory and to value real and personal property to settle Tom's estate. "Guess we'd better get started with this inventory soon as we can," said Harry. "I hate doing this. Still can't believe Tom is gone. Big funeral, wasn't it?"

John nodded. "Yeah, everyone in the whole county knew him. Damn cold weather too, but not as bad as Adria's funeral. That day she was buried was as bad as it gets."

A few minutes later Harry, the youngest of the three farmers, joined his seventy-year-old neighbors in the house. Although warmly dressed in layers with heavy overalls and wool shirts, they gathered around the roaring fire in the potbelly coal stove. The empty house still felt damp, slow to warm up. The aroma of coffee hung in the air.

"I've known Tom since my dad brought us here to homestead," said Harry. "He's one of the first people I saw when we arrived in '06. Stayed with him in his shanty that spring while my dad built our claim shack. Always neighborly."

Both men nodded in agreement.

"I've known Tom that long too. Honest, a man of his word. You could count on Tom Price," added Ed.

As an early settler, Ed had watched pioneers come and go. He began to reminisce. "Remember when we built the Robinson Hotel back in 1911, during the big boom? Yes, those were better times. Tom built the Price Livery Stable just down the street, the one he traded for this farm."

John thought back to when the new settlers' expectations ran sky high. Hope had all but vanished in thirty years.

Ed changed the subject. "How's Bruce doing?"

"Good as can be expected, I guess." said Harry. "He's in shock over losing his dad."

His companions nodded sympathetically.

"Bruce still blames himself for not coming home that weekend. But, hell, how could he know? Wasn't his fault. Bruce always boarded in town for school. Tom seemed fine when Bruce saw him that last time."

"Yes," said John, "Even if Bruce had been here, maybe he couldn't have done anything. Sometimes your time is simply up."

"John, how long do you think Tom was ailing before you came by?" asked Ed, while sipping coffee.

Slightly stooped, John eased himself into a chair, hitched up the strap of his bib overalls, and recounted in his deliberate manner what had happened. "No telling, probably that morning during chores."

"I heard he was already gone, that he froze to death."

"Nope, Tom was alive, but barely."

"One of the stories I heard was he'd been kicked by a horse," Harry added.

"Well, he had an old bruise on his body, like one of those horses might've kicked him earlier. Nobody knows when that happened."

"What a damn shame. What a way to go."

The three farmers continued drinking their strong, hot coffee in silence. John heard a team of horses approaching and looked out the kitchen window.

"Here comes Bruce now. He'll help us with the animals."

They finished their coffee while waiting for the slender seventeen-year-old, now an orphan, to stable his horses and join them. They quit talking about Tom's death in his son's presence and concentrated on the task at hand.

Judge Arnie Vinje, who'd been one of Tom Price's closest friends, had named Ed to the assessment team to inventory Tom's estate. Judge Vinje and Tom had worked together in the courthouse while Tom served as Kidder County Sheriff.

John Wilkins, another longtime neighbor, had been named the administrator, and Harry Nelson acted as Bruce's guardian. Tom's other heir, his daughter, Pearl, met the legal age and could act in her own behalf.

After a greeting and quick warmup by the fire, Bruce led the neighbors to the big red barn with its three red and white doors, faded, but still clearly painted in a checkerboard pattern.

"Let's see," said Harry making notes. "Three mares, three fillies, and two geldings. Fine animals. Tom sure had a way with horses."

The farmers noted each horse's description, including its name, and assigned an estimated value that Harry penciled on the inventory form.

Examining the striking black gelding named Pat, John noted, "From the looks of his teeth I'd say this fella is about two years old. He ought to be worth at least twenty-five dollars."

"Yes, he's exactly two years old," said Bruce. "And the three mare colts were born a year ago. See the dapple gray?" he asked, turning and pointing to the adjacent corral. "Isn't she beautiful? She's going to make a wonderful cow horse." He whistled and called to her, "C'mon Gypsy, c'mon, girl."

Gypsy immediately stopped eating hay and came trotting over, nuzzling his jacket pocket searching for a treat. "Sorry girl, not today," he said gently stroking her neck.

They continued to inventory and assign value to the livestock, thirty-four animals in all, including mature cows, yearling steers and heifers, and lastly, an Aberdeen Angus bull.

"Dad was building a Black Angus herd. Had a good start. Just needed more time," Bruce said bitterly.

The men moved on to the other buildings where they counted chickens and estimated the bushels of wheat, oats, and barley stored in the granary. They returned to the house for the noon meal of bread and cold sausages that John had volunteered to bring.

Paper and pencil in hand, they itemized the few basic household items remaining: potbellied coal heater, cook stove, a well-worn kitchen table and chairs, sturdy old dresser, and a comfortable-looking rocking chair. Two old beds, along with a cupboard, washstand, work stand, and bookcase, all made of pine, were added to the household inventory. They completed the list with a treadle sewing machine, Coronado battery-operated radio, and the nicest piece of furniture, Adria's favorite mahogany table with its graceful, flared Queen Anne legs, bought in more prosperous times.

"Lucky we hired Harold and Ivy. They'll stay here and care for the livestock and start spring planting so Bruce can finish high school, being so close to graduation," said John, refilling his cup of coffee.

Ed spoke up, "Bruce, your mother believed in education. She would've wanted you to finish."

"Yes. She'd be pleased. I just wish she was here to see it."

The group went back outdoors and continued to list and appraise Tom's aging farm machinery, tools, and equipment. Items inventoried included two sets of harnesses, haying machinery and wagons, and a wooden sled. Tom still used all the basic horse-drawn farming implements: grain box, cultivators, disc, drill, mower, binder, and John Deere sixteen-inch sulky plow with a riding seat.

One of the oldest implements was the David Bradley fourteen-inch walking plow sold by Sears, Roebuck & Company that predated his horse-drawn implements. Ed spotted it first. "Tom walked many a mile behind that plow. He busted sod for hire near Jamestown, and then used it to break virgin sod on his own homestead."

"Yes, he often talked about it. He was right proud of being the first man to ever put a plow to part of this prairie," said John.

Although intrigued with autos from their earliest days, Tom hadn't switched to farming with tractors. He stuck with the horses he knew so well. At the time of his death, Tom still owned the green 1928 Chevrolet touring car that he'd driven back and forth to California. The eleven-year-old vehicle had traveled thousands of miles on bumpy roads.

Somehow the sight of Tom's car, now well beyond its prime, evoked memories of the good old days. "Anybody remember that first Ford Tom bought about 1912?" asked Ed with a grin. "That was one of the earliest autos in northern Kidder County. Caused quite a commotion when he drove it into Robinson."

"Oh yes," said Harry laughing. "I remember it well. Big and black and shiny. I still recall Tom gave my brother and me a ride. I wanted to learn to drive it, but my dad wouldn't hear of it." Bruce laughed. He'd heard his dad's car stories many times.

Their task complete, the men returned to the house. Harry tallied the value of the appraisal. "$1200."

After a brief silence, Harry spoke out loud what the others were probably thinking, "Sure isn't much to show for a lifetime of hard work, is it? If it hadn't been for the damn Depression, he'd have done just fine. Think I need a stiff drink."

Tom's land had been heavily mortgaged when its value sharply dropped in the '30s. There simply hadn't been enough farm income for a decade. The Prices borrowed to purchase the barest essentials. Tom hadn't paid taxes for six years, fully aware of the possible consequences. As county sheriff, his duties had included holding numerous foreclosure sales, no matter how personally distasteful.

Within a couple years of his death, Tom Price's heirs lost the land, more than 720 acres that included his and Adria's original homesteads, to mortgage foreclosure and delinquent taxes.

In the final accounting, after auctioning most of his farm possessions, clearing his charge accounts at the local merchants, and paying his legal, medical, and funeral expenses, Tom Price's estate consisted of just sixty-two dollars and twenty-five cents. The meager sum was split between Pearl and Bruce.

Bruce found himself suddenly on his own. He abandoned any hopes for post-high-school education. Bruce idolized his father and figuratively walked in Tom's boots, even if they were impossibly large. Young and optimistic, he charted his future course. Bruce, like his father before him, chose the land. He now worked to fulfill his father's dreams.

Wedding photo of Bruce and Evelyn (Shirley) Price.

PART II

Second Generation: Bruce and Evelyn Come of Age

Bruce and Evelyn had long been considered a couple, often seen attending movies and dances together throughout the county. When they decided to marry, Bruce wrote to his older married sister, Pearl, asking about legal requirements. Pearl kept the letter and produced it years later, much to my Dad's embarrassment.

In his letter the prospective groom raised several concerns. "Where do you get your blood test? How many days must you wait? Where is the best place to get a ring?" he inquired.

Bruce asked his sister to help him clean up the farmhouse where he'd been living. Before he brought his new bride home, he also asked Pearl to bring an iron along to press his white shirt and suit. He admonished her to keep the wedding plans "on the QT" (in secret) just to see if they could. Meanwhile the couple quietly applied for a marriage license, made an appointment with clergy, and completed their required blood tests in Steele without telling their friends.

Of course, unless they lived the remote lives of hermits, the couple had no possibility of privacy in their rural community. Someone always observed and gossiped. Perhaps it was simply the desire to be the first to learn news, good or bad. Since it was nearly impossible to keep a secret, Evelyn and Bruce decided to try.

With money tight, the wedding would be private. Just their immediate family knew of their wedding plans; the only risk was someone spotting Bruce picking out the ring in Bismarck. They arranged to have Pearl, living near Steele, go to the doctor's office and obtain their medical test results. When the tests came back as expected, Pearl left a prearranged, coded message for Bruce with the Robinson community telephone operator.

"Tell Bruce his wind charger parts have arrived in Steele," Pearl told the operator. The operator dutifully passed on the mundane message the next time Bruce came to Robinson.

"Thanks. I'll head down there to pick them up," he said, stifling a laugh. He knew that meant the wedding could proceed on schedule.

Evelyn Shirley, eighteen, and Bruce Arthur Price, twenty-one, were married by a Lutheran minister in Steele on January 27, 1943, at high noon. Pearl and her husband, Emil Janke, as well as Evelyn's sister, Agnes Shirley, attended the wedding ceremony held in the parsonage. Evelyn wore a store-bought beige, two-piece wool suit, and Bruce donned his freshly pressed, gray pinstripe suit. After the brief ceremony they stopped for coffee at the local cafe where they spotted Bruce and Pearl's uncle, Ed Williams. Bruce waved the gentlemen over, "Hey Ed, be the first to meet my new wife, Evelyn Price."

Ed grinned and extended a congratulatory hand to the self-conscious bride. "Welcome to the family." The wedding party then drove the twenty-five miles to Evelyn's home where Petra had remained to prepare a feast in celebration of her daughter's nuptials.

Evelyn and Bruce announced their marriage in the newspaper, surprising many townspeople. They settled into life together in the tiny white house on the Checkerboard Farm.

Bruce often kidded Evelyn about picking such a bitterly cold wedding day—the thermometer registered minus twenty-six degrees Fahrenheit that morning. I can still hear him spin the tale. "I said we'd get married in Steele that next Wednesday, if my car would start. And, wouldn't you know it, of all days, that damn car started on the first try. That old clunker never started in January, I could guarantee it. But I gave my word, and I had to keep it," he'd say with a wink and a wicked grin.

A few nights after the wedding, their friends playfully shivareed the newlyweds, waking them up at their farm with a hubbub of noise and a mock serenade. The visitors demanded refreshments and generally harassed the couple.

The community ladies later threw a double wedding shower for Evelyn and her new sister-in-law, Peggy Shirley, Glen's wife. The two newlywed couples in turn hosted a public wedding dance. Because of wartime gas rationing and tire shortages, an outside band they wanted to hire was unable to drive to Robinson. Instead, the hosts temporarily moved the nickelodeon from the bar to the dance hall. The source of the music didn't matter. Community guests of all ages waltzed and two-stepped into the wee morning hours.

◆   ◆   ◆

Bruce had already chosen to remain on the family land. In 1941, when Tom's land had come up for sale at public auction for unpaid taxes, neighbors supported Bruce's decision to buy back the farm. Applying social pressure, they discouraged outsiders from bidding against Bruce on the land and running up the value.

"Give the boy a chance. He wants to farm," neighbors pleaded at the auction sale. The strategy worked. It allowed Bruce to use a loan from his mother's brothers to buy the family farm back at a reduced price and pay off the taxes. Without that help, the land would have been lost to taxes.

Pearl generously relinquished her inherited share of the land to Bruce so the farm would remain intact and economically viable. Bruce never forgot Pearl's generosity. They remained close their entire lives.

Once Bruce attained his full legal majority, he could transact his own business. Although he began farming deeply in debt, paying off the debts his father owed at the time of Tom's untimely death became a high priority. After a few years Bruce announced with pride that he had "cleared the Price name."

Meanwhile, Evelyn and Bruce's first-born, a healthy son named Dennis Arthur, arrived in October of 1944. His middle name honored both his father and grandfather. The young family, though poor, felt blessed. They now had an heir who could inherit the land.

Bruce Price holding Dennis.

It's a Girl!

A year and a half later on April 30, 1946, my birth caused quite a stir at St. Alexius Hospital in Bismarck on the eve of Baby Week. A promotion sponsored by city merchants who capitalized on the beginning of the post-war baby boom promised to shower a lucky baby with gifts of equipment and clothing. Because I was the only newborn delivered—with no one else in labor—the nurses assured my mother, Evelyn, I would be the Baby Week prizewinner. My mother allowed herself to dream of collecting wonderful gifts and getting our picture in the Bismarck paper.

Judy Rae Price as infant.

But alas, a baby born in the next hospital claimed the prize. So much for fifteen minutes of fame! Instead, I came home in obscurity to a loving family who had precious little in the way of material wealth, but considerable optimism.

My folks rejoiced at a healthy, seven-and-a-half pound daughter, but trouble loomed. I thrived for the first months, but when Mom introduced me to solid foods, she discovered I was unable to swallow anything unless it was liquefied.

I periodically vomited up all food and drink and begin to lose weight. I became dehydrated. Some days I'd swallow pureed foods, but on other days I'd show distress and try to trigger a vomiting reflex, sticking my tiny hand into my mouth. My mother used her fingers to induce vomiting, to my obvious relief.

At first the doctors dismissed my intermittent vomiting as teething. As this condition dragged on, my folks became terrified. They had no medical insurance or savings, so I became a financial burden. The doctors remained perplexed, as I was otherwise healthy. My condition didn't improve. As I approached my first birthday, my weight fell to a dangerous twelve pounds. I was hospitalized and fed intravenously to regain weight. Meanwhile townsfolk began whispering, "That child is going to die if she can't eat. They can't feed her with a tube her whole life."

Doctors suspected a stricture (blockage) or narrowing of the esophagus, but no one knew how to correct the condition in an infant. The future looked bleak. I was referred to the prestigious Mayo Clinic in Rochester, Minnesota. My folks took out loans to pay the mounting doctor and hospital bills. Cash upfront always preceded hospital services.

We headed to Minnesota on the first plane trip for both my parents and me, while relatives cared for Dennis, still a toddler. My father suffered from severe motion sickness. By the time Dad climbed out of the propeller plane, the driver from the hospital thought my father was the inbound patient.

The specialists at Mayo Clinic performed an esophagoscopy and discovered what they assumed was a congenital partial blockage. They then dilated the food tube with an instrument to stretch it open. Strapping me down and forcing me to swallow thread with an instrument attached accomplished this.

The dilation helped, and I swallowed again. They discharged me, hoping the esophagus would stay open. A few weeks later the cycle started again. The only other prospect, besides repeated dilation, was the possibility of experimental operations to surgically enlarge my esophagus as I grew. My family dreaded subjecting me to painful procedures or repeat surgeries. Plus, they had no idea how they would pay for additional hospitalizations.

They returned home heavy-hearted and struggled to make a decision. What irony: They had grown food for the war effort and now the European recovery, and yet their own baby faced starvation.

Meanwhile, the farming community had turned out en masse to plant our crops while my parents were preoccupied with my hospitalization. This demonstrated the best of rural life—neighbors taking care of their own. My folks often told me how grateful they felt toward those neighbors.

A few relatives knew that my paternal grandmother had lost an infant brother who couldn't swallow. "Maybe it's the same condition," they speculated. They hoped access to modern medicine could prevent the same fate for me.

Finally, in a desperate effort to avoid more surgery, my skeptical parents tried a friend's recommendation and brought me to a chiropractor in a nearby town. As they explained to me later, what did they have to lose?

The chiropractor performed painless manipulations to vertebrae in the thoracic area of my spine. This apparently relieved the nerve spasms in the esophagus. Amazingly, my food tube opened up, and I began to eat solids and regain my strength.

Over the next five years, my food tube often closed, triggered by bulky food that would get painfully stuck. I'd usually clear the obstruction by vomiting. Unfortunately, my windpipe sometimes became involved, and I faced serious breathing difficulty. They'd rush me to that chiropractor for a spinal manipulation to stop the spasms. Each time, I'd resume normal breathing and eating soon after a treatment.

My folks closely monitored the type of food I ate, and taught me to chew thoroughly. During my preschool years, hard-to-swallow foods such as corn, peanuts, or hard candies were forbidden. Candy bars were problematic because nearly all contained nuts. Mr. Swanson, the local grocer, kindly set aside a plain Hershey candy bar for me whenever a shipment arrived. He knew it was the only candy I could swallow.

One evening, I signaled to my mother that something was stuck in my chest. Because I was only sixteen months old, I can't remember the incident. Mom said she tried the usual practice drill, patting me on the back, with no relief. She and her hired kitchen helpers had just finished an exhausting day, cooking and serving three huge meals for a harvest crew. None of the ladies saw me eat anything abnormal, but Mom worried I might have swallowed forbidden food.

Dad was exhausted from directing the harvesting of his ripe wheat before any rain might interfere. Although I didn't cry that evening, I couldn't eat or drink before going to sleep. Worried, Mom checked my breathing throughout the night. When I began choking and gagging at breakfast with serious breathing difficulties, they decided to seek medical help.

My folks left others in charge of the harvest and rushed me by car to our chiropractor, an hour away. He took a chest X-ray while I lay listless on the table, my breathing deteriorating. The X-ray appeared normal, yet I was obviously in distress. The chiropractor performed his usual spine manipulation, but this time nothing happened. Alarmed I might need surgical intervention for my breathing, the chiropractor sent us rushing to a medical doctor, just a few doors down the street.

The chiropractor asked my parents not to disclose to the medical doctor that we had first sought his services. Physicians typically displayed animosity toward alternative medicine, and the medical doctor considered the chiropractor a quack.

Mom ran on ahead, jostling me up and down as she carried me, the heels of her dress shoes clicking hard on the sidewalk. Dad with his longer strides followed close behind, carrying her purse and bags. The other patients in the waiting room stared at us as we entered. The nurse with her starched white cap took one look at my pale body, limp as a Raggedy Ann doll, and ushered us into a treatment room. "I'll interrupt the doctor," she said.

Within minutes of arriving in the office, while the doctor began questioning my folks, I became agitated, indicating something was stuck. Mom bent me over her arm and pounded me hard twice on the back. A two-inch-long chunk of bologna ejected and shot across the room, landing under the doctor's chair. The meat had not been visible in the X-ray.

"Oh, my goodness," gasped my mother, "I served bologna for supper last night. A thresher must have given it to her or she picked it up herself."

My color quickly returned to normal, and I drank water, which I could now swallow. "Amazing! Thank God," Dad said, grinning from ear to ear. I began to explore the office, and asked for food with my limited vocabulary.

The physician watching me took off his reading glasses and laughed heartily. "I've never seen anything like it," he said. "She's fine. Take her home and enjoy her. No charge for you folks. I didn't do anything."

We exited through the physician's waiting room, this time with me walking and smiling while holding my father's hand. The strangers in the room acted as if they'd seen a miracle. They clapped and cheered as we made our way out the door. The beaming doctor followed behind us. Addressing the room with a broad grin, he asked, "Anyone else?" People laughed, wishing for their own miracle.

Dad took us straight to the drug store and ordered malted milks. I downed mine while Dad reported back to the chiropractor. My father had respected the chiropractor's request but wanted him to know the happy outcome. Then we hurried back to Dad's grain fields, alive with harvesting men and equipment.

◆   ◆   ◆

The congenital swallowing difficulty steadily improved, but I still had problems. Three years later, as the story goes, when I was four, I confessed to my mother, "I swallowed something, and it's stuck."

"What?"

"A garter."

She was skeptical. "Show me."

Going to the laundry basket, I pointed to a small metal fastener that attached ladies' hose to a belt or corset.

"Oh, no. Why did you put that in your mouth?" she asked, her face getting red.

I began to cry. "It's stuck and it hurts."

Back we went to the chiropractor. The X-ray revealed the metal object, so he knew I'd need surgery. He sent us by small plane to a hospital in Minot, eighty miles farther away. When we arrived at the hospital they changed me into pajamas so big I could barely see my hands and feet. A doctor in a white coat forced me to swallow terrible-tasting string with a tool attached to it. My throat ached. Then, the doctor said to my folks, "Time for you to leave."

I clearly remember that I begged, "Please don't go. Please stay." But they hugged me and went away, leaving me with those strangers.

A man wearing a green top and pants put me on a cold metal table and pushed it into a scary room. Some of the operating equipment looked like a giant kitchen stove. The bright lights in the ceiling hurt my eyes. I tried to wiggle away and escape, but they held me down. Now I really needed my mother. "Mommy, Mommy," I screeched, choking and coughing, terrified. But no one came. I felt abandoned.

More nurses entered the room wearing masks. My hopes soared when I recognized one behind her mask. It was Joyce, my grown-up cousin. I begged her for assistance, but she wouldn't help. Joyce just stood there and said, "Don't cry, Judy, It's going to be okay." Then a man wearing a mask held a smelly washcloth over my nose and mouth. The lights went out.

I woke up feeling strange. I lay in a crib in a different room with animal pictures on the wall. I wore different pajamas and a diaper. I didn't need a diaper! I fussed to the nurses about the diaper, but they didn't let me change. I thought Mommy could tell them, but she wasn't around. I just wanted out.

"Are you hungry?" a nurse wearing white asked, offering me spoonfuls of red Jell-O. I tried to eat, but my throat and my head hurt. A doctor stopped by to look down my throat. I didn't like doctors any more. They hurt me.

I felt homesick and started to sob. Another lady in blue came in with two cardboard picture books. "I have fuzzy books," she said. She showed me the animal pictures and rubbed my fingers over the fuzzy parts. "I don't care," I told her, still crying. "I want to go home. I want Mommy and Daddy." I threw the books on the floor.

Then my cousin Joyce came by, wearing that special white dress and cap and shoes, but no mask this time. She told me she'd talked to my folks. "They're coming to get you soon," she said, which consoled me. I complained about the diaper, and Joyce let me change. "You'll be going home, so you can get dressed in your own clothes, but you have to wait in bed until they come." She and the other nurse made me a hair bow out of gauze bandages decorated with red Mercurochrome dots. Next Joyce brought me vanilla ice cream, which felt cool on my aching throat.

When my folks arrived, I put on my MaryJane shoes and we left. The noisy plane ride kept me awake, but the long car ride made me sleepy. When we arrived home, I told my brother I wanted to become a nurse so I could wear one of those fancy white caps.

◆   ◆   ◆

Just after I celebrated my fifth birthday, my beloved grandmother, Petra Shirley, died. It made me sad to see Mommy cry. Children didn't go to funerals, but my mother took Dennis and me to the church to say goodbye to Grandma in the lavender casket before the funeral began. Grandma wore her blue and white polka dot dress, but I didn't think she looked right. Her skin was an odd color, and she was wearing lipstick. Grandma never wore lipstick! Bunches of strong-smelling, burgundy roses stood nearby. To this day the cloyingly sweet smell of a certain deep red rose triggers a memory and brings back the image of Grandma in her casket.

The sight of her lying in that purple box frightened me. I knew she couldn't wake up. My folks told us Grandma was going to heaven, but I didn't understand how she would get there and kept watching the sky. We stayed with a babysitter while Mom and Dad went to the services and cemetery. I felt miserable, too upset to play or eat.

The next morning I tried to eat, but couldn't swallow anything, even water. I gagged and had trouble breathing. My folks dropped everything and called on a neighbor, Glen Whitman, to fly us to the chiropractor in his airplane.

My parents enlisted Aunt Kay, who was visiting, to baby-sit my brothers. Someone drove to the nearest phone in town and called the chiropractor, alerting him we were on the way. The chiropractor met us at the airport. He manipulated my spine, and I stopped choking and breathed easier. Nothing had stuck in my esophagus this time. He thought the shock of my grandmother's death caused my nerves to spasm.

"Mrs. Price, let me show you what to do if this happens again, and you can't get here," the chiropractor said. He guided her fingers on my upper spine, showing her exactly where to gently push. Mom later said the chiropractor had what she called a "premonition," because he died soon after that visit. Fortunately, I never again needed his services.

As I matured during first and second grade, the condition steadily improved. However, if I rushed through lunch, the food got stuck in my esophagus, and I'd go to the girls' lavatory to bring it up. My brother couldn't assist because our restroom remained off limits to boys. We had no school nurse, and my teacher couldn't leave the classroom unattended, so my cousin, Linda, just two years older, accompanied me and made sure I recovered. Without a phone to notify her, Mom was powerless to help me.

A Day That Changed Our Lives

On September 6, 1950, my whole world changed forever. My brother, Dale, was born that day. With the new baby's homecoming, my role in the family shifted from little sis to self-appointed, four-year-old "junior mom."

Grandpa Gust carried the new baby into the farmhouse in a white wicker bassinet. He had accompanied my dad on the sixty-five-mile trip to Bismarck hospital to pick up Mom and the new arrival. Quickly brushing past my mother with a "Hi, Mommy," I anxiously looked at this newcomer. His little face and tiny hands fascinated me.

"Why is he so red?" I asked, peering deep into the blue blanket. "I thought Daddy said he was a big baby." Even wrapped in a bulky blanket, nine pounds and three ounces looked tiny to me.

"Oh, he's big for a new baby," Mom assured me giving me a long hug, "and all babies look red at first."

Six-year-old Dennis had wanted a brother, but I'd hoped for a sister. "But Mommy," I said, "Dennis got a brother. He keeps teasing me 'cause he won."

"Oh, it doesn't really matter," my mother said. "You'll like having another brother." Mom proved to be right.

I began dividing my time and attention between my two siblings, helping look after one and sharing secrets with the other. Growing up as the middle child and the only girl, I eventually found myself faced with choosing sides between two unique brothers with different temperaments. Later I became their go-between and often their mediator, a role I played all my life.

Dennis, Judy, and Dale Price.

◆   ◆   ◆

That September day also proved memorable because Dad drove Dennis to his first day at school, leaving me with a babysitter. He then headed for the hospital.

Dennis had been my sole playmate, so I felt abandoned when he started first grade. The closest neighbor children lived three miles away. Envious, I didn't understand why I couldn't go along to school with him. With no other children around, I grew lonely on the farm.

The cats, tame enough to allow Dennis and me to dress them in doll clothes and push them in a doll buggy, now became my main playmates when he was at school. None of our cats were spayed or neutered, so eventually kittens overran the farm. Dad quietly disposed of all but one or two from each litter, if he discovered them before we did. Otherwise, we tamed them.

We hand-raised one white kitten, Snowball, from infancy. While driving a tractor, Dad inadvertently hit its mother, a stray living in the fields. My father noticed the victim had been nursing and looked for her litter. He rescued one kitten, and then drowned the remaining newborns to prevent them from slowly starving.

We took turns feeding tiny Snowball every few hours around the clock using a doll bottle and warm cow's milk. Although the odds were against it, the kitten survived and became a fascinating pet. Our cats had died from distemper earlier that year, so Snowball missed early imprinting by cats. Instead the white kitten imitated our German Shepherd dog and had no clue how to hunt like a cat. We fed him cow's milk and table scraps. Our Snowball lived a pampered life to an old age.

One of the activities Dennis and I had enjoyed together as preschoolers was playing with mud. We molded cakes and pies by pressing the gooey mud into aluminum, child-sized baking pans and letting it harden in the sun. Then someone—no doubt the eldest—got the bright idea of using fresh eggs from the chicken coop to bind the mud, so it would retain its shape after we removed the baking pans. I liked the way eggs made the frosting shiny. We got caught when Mom saw the cats licking our muddy confections. A quick search yielded several broken eggshells near our play area.

Once Dennis and I built an elaborate makeshift playhouse with castoff wood and metal pieces from Dad's workshop. We stocked it with toy dishes and odds and ends we used as pretend food. This project kept us busy for weeks, and we proudly displayed our creativity to anyone stopping by the farm.

One day, Mr. Sando, the nearly deaf trucker, came by to deliver coal with his big dump truck. We quit playing to watch him from a safe distance as he dumped his dusty load into our coal bin. When finished, he made a wide U-turn in the yard. He then shifted his big truck in reverse and backed right over our playhouse. He re-shifted, grinding the gears noisily and lumbered off, never looking back. In an instant, the old man destroyed all our hard work. Our playhouse was trashed.

The noise of the crash brought Mom outside. "What happened"?

"Mommy, he ruined our playhouse!" I cried.

"Who did?"

"That old man in the truck. He drove right over it and broke all our dishes," I said holding up a shard of pottery and a flattened cake pan.

"Well, thank God you weren't playing in it. We can get more dishes," she said shuddering. She gave us each a tight hug. "I'm so happy you weren't hurt. You could've been run over. I'll talk to Dad about Sando's driving."

Years later I learned that many people worried about the old bachelor's bad driving. Sando never hit anyone, but had caused so many fender-benders that no one risked riding with him. Dad refused to allow him to drive into our yard after the incident, and personally maneuvered Sando's truck whenever the old man delivered coal.

I stayed mad a long time over losing my dishes. At Christmas I wrote Santa to bring me new ones, and he delivered. My new tin set had a Blue Willow design.

I enjoyed playing with Dennis' toys, such as trucks and building blocks, but I loved playing with dolls. One day I left my favorite doll, made of soft rubber, out in the hot sun. Her arm partially melted at the elbow. My quick-thinking mother came to the rescue and created a cloth sling that covered the damage. Now I had a patient with a permanent broken arm when I played nurse.

My child's medical kit came complete with pretend stethoscope, white cap, and red cape. I coaxed Dennis into playing hospital using my dolls as patients. True to the times, he played the doctor, while I acted as chief nurse. We enlisted kittens as patients. They kept escaping from our cardboard hospital. We didn't need a stethoscope to hear their hearts pounding as they ran away.

◆　　◆　　◆

"I predict Dennis will grow up to be a doctor," teased Dad. "Maybe he'll work on artificial limbs."

Dad loved to tell the tale. When my brother, Dennis, was two, an elderly lady called on Aunt Hilda while little Dennis was visiting there. The ladies chatted over coffee and homemade cake while Dennis entertained himself underfoot with a favorite toy, a small wooden peg and hammer set. Adept at pounding, Dennis knocked the pegs flush with their platform with a few quick strokes of the wooden mallet.

Suddenly the hammer made a sickeningly hollow sound. Bong.

Dennis knew he'd hit the lady's leg. He dropped the mallet and cowered in fear, the color drained from his face. "It's all right, honey," the victim said, trying to reassure him, "It didn't hurt."

Dennis remained unconvinced. The well-meaning lady continued, "Here, let me show you." She reached under her long flowered dress and unhooked her wooden leg at the knee. She held the leg up high for his inspection. "See. It comes off."

That did it. The terrified boy ran screaming from the room. He crawled under the bed and refused to come out until she had left. He wouldn't touch the toy hammer for weeks.

◆　　◆　　◆

Before my brother was born, Mom decided to pass along her only childhood doll to me. The composition-type doll, common in the 1920s, was the size of a real infant. Its ceramic hands, feet, head, and shoulder plate attached to a squarish cloth body that could be posed to sit or lie down.

Mom's prize doll had been lovingly cared for, and had only minor cracking of the glaze on her face. As a girl, Mom had stitched colorful cotton dresses for her.

In my four-year-old worldview, I dismissed the "olden days" doll and her dresses as old fashioned. She wasn't slim like my baby dolls. Much to my mother's chagrin, I insisted on naming the doll after a favorite aunt with an apple-shaped body type, and then told everyone why I chose that name. Only later did I grow to appreciate the doll from my Mom's childhood.

I dreamed of dolls I saw in the Sears Wish Book, as we called their Christmas catalog. I filled out extensive Sears order forms for Santa. I also played with paper dolls, which predated Barbie fashion dolls. They were constructed of heavy cardboard with platforms to stand upright. Little paper tabs hooked the fancy paper costumes to the dolls. My favorites were the stars of the day, Dale Evans, Grace Kelly, or Lucille Ball.

One Christmas, Mom surprised me with a white satin and lace bridal gown for my doll, made while I attended school. She stitched a mint green organdy bridesmaid gown for a second doll. I was thrilled. It must have been difficult to hide every scrap of lace from my inquisitive eyes. She later confided, "I hid the bag of sewing materials inside the washing machine."

◆   ◆   ◆

A third momentous event occurred on September 6, 1950. We finally joined the rest of the country in gaining electricity. More than a couple decades late, we converted from battery power to electrical power.

We'd been watching linemen putting up tall poles and stringing wire leading to our farm. Electricians wired our house. Dad, although thankful to get electricity, complained about how much it would cost to change over. In spite of subsidies, the expense of providing electrical power to widely scattered individual farms had delayed its arrival. Our village friends, and those farmers in close proximity to them, had long enjoyed electrical power. Telephones for farmers remained years away, for the same economic reasons. When we finally got phones, we used a seven-family party line with no privacy whatsoever. Today, in the cell-phone era, this seems unimaginable.

With the advent of electricity, the workday changed for my mother. Methods of cooking and doing laundry improved. Over time we bought electric lamps, a toaster, a fancy steam iron, a modern radio, and a wringer washing machine.

Mom immediately lobbied for a refrigerator. With no ice delivery route or commercial source of ice, we'd never owned an icebox. In the winter Mother Nature provided a natural icebox, albeit with no temperature controls. We got fresh milk from our dairy cows each morning and evening. In the summer, all Mom could do to chill it was to lower a small covered bucket of perishables into the family well via a rope.

I heard my folks arguing. "A refrigerator would make it easier to keep the baby's food and milk bottles from spoiling in the heat," Mom said. "It'd save me time to store perishables in the kitchen instead of lowering them into the well. Please, let's get a refrigerator right away," she pleaded with Dad.

My father suggested an alternate plan. "If we buy a freezer instead, we can store the meat at home after we butcher," he argued. I can picture Dad salivating just thinking of thick, juicy steaks. Because he raised cattle and pigs, Dad insisted on red meat twice a day.

"What about ice cream?" Dad asked. His favorite dessert was store-bought ice cream. "We could eat ice cream anytime we wanted it," he said. Dad won the argument. He purchased a new chest-style freezer to hold our home-grown beef and pork as well as the venison and pheasants he hunted. He no longer needed to rent cold storage lockers in Tuttle, ten miles away.

Money remained tight, so Mom didn't get the refrigerator she wanted for a whole year, until after we sold the next fall's wheat harvest. Somehow Mom continued to cook three full meals a day for her growing family without any convenient method of keeping food chilled.

Our house had no basement, just a root cellar to store vegetables. The cellar, off limits to us, looked dark and scary. That made us all the more curious as to what might live down there. We imagined bogeymen and wild animals lurking in the dark. We cautiously peered over the edge of the trap door as Mom or Dad descended by a crude wooden ladder into a dark, dank-smelling pit.

"Stay back, kids. Don't get too close to the edge," Dad reminded us one day. Too late! I leaned over just a wee bit too far, and plunged into the darkness. Fortunately, my father remained at the base of the six-foot ladder as he reached for the lantern. Somehow he managed to catch me in his arms. After that terrifying event, I stayed well back from the edge while he or Mom retrieved food, letting them cope with the dangers of the dungeon.

Television Expands Our World

My godparents, Mabel and Art Bon, made me feel special. Since I'd lost my only grandmother early, Mabel became my surrogate grandmother. She wore a clean printed housedress and apron and carried a flowered cloth handkerchief. I picture her showing us the newest blooms in her flower garden or serving us cookies. She always smiled.

The Bons took us with them on errands and bought us gifts. I treasured the books they gave me, such as *Cinderella*, *Little Women*, and *Five Little Peppers and How They Grew*. Art took home movies of us and let us watch ourselves on screen. We looked forward to visiting them on their farm, about two-and-a-half miles away. They always had a new baby animal to check out or perhaps a lamb to feed. Mabel and Art both died while I was in high school.

I remember seeing my first glimpse of television, a big black box with a tiny screen, while visiting the Bons in about 1953. Art was the first person we knew to purchase the new technology. My family gathered around to check out this novelty that would eventually transform our leisure habits. I was fascinated to see the Bismarck radio announcers on television. Dad was intrigued, determined he would buy a set.

Our neighbor had erected a huge antenna that could capture the signals beamed from seventy miles to the west or 100 miles to the east. We watched the fuzzy black-and-white program until a test pattern appeared at sign off. Dennis and I wished we lived closer to this magic box.

A year or two later, Dad surprised our family with our first television set. Ecstatic, we helped rearrange the crowded living room to accommodate the bulky set. Radio became secondary, now relegated to news and weather reports.

We received reliable signals from NBC, and if weather permitted, from CBS. Dad went outside and physically rotated the antenna with a hand crank he had installed on the tall pole next to the house. "How's that? Snowy? Okay. I'll leave it right here," Dad yelled through the open door as he adjusted the antenna to find the optimum position. In stormy weather conditions we were lucky to get one channel.

By the time I was old enough to enjoy movies, Robinson's theater had closed. The one movie I recall seeing with my family at the Steele cinema was the colorful epic, *The Ten Commandments*. Television opened a new world. Having access to entertainment was wonderful, despite the grainy black and white picture. At first television played for a limited number of hours each day. The programming ended with the national anthem.

The entire family watched the same television programs together in the days before remote controls or additional sets. "Hey, Dad, we want to watch Disneyland," we pleaded.

At times Dad preempted the debate, for example, when he watched boxing on the *Friday Night Fights* or the popular quiz show *The $64,000 Question*. Family favorites included *Wagon Train*, *I Love Lucy*, and *The Ed Sullivan Show*. Dad grumbled when he first saw Elvis on the Sullivan show. I especially liked *Your Hit Parade*. Dad taught me to dance to the television music of North Dakota's favorite son, Lawrence Welk.

Our childhood heroes were western movie stars, like Roy Rogers and Dale Evans. Other favorites included Hopalong Cassidy, the Lone Ranger, Davy Crockett, and Zorro. *The Mickey Mouse Club* reigned after school and cartoons played on Saturday morning. We coveted lunch pails sporting Roy Rogers, Dale Evans, or the Lone Ranger. Merchandising had arrived.

Dennis and I spent our preschool years without television, so we were envious of Dale. He grew up with Buffalo Bob and Howdy Dowdy, as well as Captain Kangaroo. Mom helped Dale claim his official deputy sheriff membership card from a children's show originating in Bismarck.

We proudly wore western hats and toy six-guns. Mom took outdoor photos of my brothers at Christmastime with guns and holsters slung over bulky snowsuits. Somehow I can't imagine Roy Rogers wearing a snowsuit.

Snow

During the winter of 1950–51, we endured record-breaking snowfall that isolated us on the farm. Snowdrifts blocked our unimproved dirt roads. Driving a car or truck became impossible.

My folks arranged for Dennis to stay with a family in the village while attending first grade there. During the heaviest snowfall, Dennis remained "snowed away" for six long weeks. My father traveled the five-and-a-half mile trek to visit Dennis by horse and wagon whenever he bought supplies. Mom, baby Dale, and I stayed home. With no telephone, we had no outside contact, just the radio. The baby mostly ate and slept. Mom spent a lot of time reading Golden Books to me and teaching me songs. When I grew lonely for Dennis, I colored pictures for Dad to deliver to him. The cats were not allowed in the house, so they stayed in the shelter of the barn during the coldest days.

"Judy, look up," Dad said one morning while excitedly pointing to the sky through the kitchen window. I ran over in time to see an airplane drop a canvas bag from the sky.

"What's that? What's the plane doing, Daddy?"

"They're dropping our mail."

The excitement mounted as we watched the neighbor's yellow Piper Cub circle our farm once more to get our attention. They wanted to alert us that the mail had been dropped. Dad opened the kitchen door and waved broadly, signaling the pilot. As the blast of cold air spread through the kitchen, the plane headed to the next farm.

"You wait here," Dad said, pulling on his four-buckle overshoes, heavy coat, hat, and gloves and headed outdoors. Mom and I watched as he broke a path through the tall snowbanks to retrieve the heavy bag. It had landed in a snowy field just south of the farmstead. The bag contained weeks of mail and newspapers and a package ordered from Sears. Snow-blocked roads—including the railroads—had prevented delivery to our town's post office. Glen Whitman, a local farmer and pilot, flew to Jamestown to secure mail for the entire Robinson area. He and the mail carrier, Harold Bullis, then delivered to individual farms via our own "airmail" route.

My earliest winter recollections include biting cold, bulky snowsuits, impossible-to-pull-on boots, red runny noses, snowballs, and that pungent, musty smell of wet woolen mittens. Mom attached our mittens to our snowsuit sleeves with big safety pins. "Now don't lose your mittens," she'd say. We still managed to come up one mitten short, which we didn't find until the snow melted in the spring.

Dennis and I often played outside on sunny winter days, temperature permitting. "Let's play fox and goose," Dennis suggested. He began stamping out a large circular path in the new-fallen snow and challenged me to chase him.

"Just a minute," I said, occupied with my own project. From a standing position, I fell straight backward on the clean carpet of snow and fully extended my arms and legs. While still lying in the snow, I swung my limbs back and forth. Carefully getting up, I jumped outside the familiar celestial shape to avoid any telltale footprints, and stood back to admire my artwork.

"Look at my snow angel," I said proudly pointing to the shape I had created in the sparkling white carpet. "I make the best ones," I boasted, dusting the loose snow off my fuchsia snow pants and jacket.

Usually the snow felt dry and powdery, but when it contained enough moisture content, Dennis and I would build a snowman. We'd each form a snowball and roll it across the drifts, racing to see who could make it bigger. We'd stack three of them atop each other, starting with the largest on the bottom, making him as tall as we could reach.

"Let's call him Frosty, just like in the song," I said, humming the popular tune.

"Find some gravel," Dennis suggested. We scrounged the snow-dusted farmyard for chunks of coal or gravel stones to use for eyes. Stones proved handy as buttons marching down Frosty's chest. Next we asked Mom for a potato or carrot for his nose. We didn't have many trees, but we found small twigs for arms. Mom lent us a hat for our Frosty to wear over his straw hair.

"Hey, go tell Mom Frosty needs mittens," Dennis said, trying to keep the "buttons" from slipping out of place.

But I had a better idea. "He can wear mine. They're all wet anyway."

We grew up before snowmobiles became common. Our rides were limited to our wooden Flexible Flyer sled. The land was mostly level, so we didn't have long hills for coasting. We used the sled on the steep sides of the road ditches, but the danger of barbed wire fences obscured with snow made some areas off-limits.

One storm left unusually high snowdrifts blown around the farm buildings. That enabled us to climb all the way to the rooftop of Dad's shop on the packed snow. Dennis noticed the snow would make a great ramp, so we dragged the wagon to the top of the wooden roof.

"You go first," Dennis said. "Get in and go straight across to the other side. You'll coast all the way down the long snowbank. I'll push to get you started."

"Okay." It sounded like a good plan to me. At four, I was gullible and usually followed my big brother's instructions. I climbed into the wagon, and Dennis pushed me to gain momentum. I planned to follow the long, snow-packed ramp, gracefully gliding all the way across the yard. Unfortunately, I wasn't adept at steering.

In the excitement, I managed to go crossways, about 180 degrees off-target. The wagon left the roof at the far corner rather than the side with the tall snowbank. As I tried to correct the steering, the wagon jackknifed and the back axle caught on the corner of the eave. I tumbled headfirst into a narrow windswept hole between the snowdrifts and the corner of the building. The now-vertical wagon hung precariously over me, ten feet above the ground.

Dennis ran yelling for help, and it took a rescue effort by Dad with a ladder to extricate me. I emerged, shaken but unhurt. Dad looked angry. He declared, "No more climbing on the roof, you two. Do you understand? Don't ever take the wagon up there again."

My joy in new-fallen snow turned out to be short-lived. The older I got, the less I liked snow. I noticed that the clean carpet of powdery snow quickly gave way to brownish murky piles only partly covering the bare, frozen earth. It turned brown and gritty, mixed with gravel and soil, or it formed deep ruts. We learned to avoid animal droppings and knew we should never, ever taste yellow snow. As a child I thought the big snow piles lasted forever, but eventually they evaporated in the sunshine or melted into cold, slushy puddles.

I must have internalized my Dad's negative response to winter. He personally knew the dangers of cold. Each winter night before retiring, Dad checked the outdoor thermometer mounted near the window. His cussing rose as the mercury fell to twenty or thirty degrees below zero, without calculating the wind chill factor. "It's going to be damn cold tonight!"

Although I rarely had to shovel, I disliked the travel restrictions snow caused. For Dad, cold and snow meant shoveling and additional work protecting the animals. "Can't get that cold-blooded truck started," he used to grumble. "Don't have time to fight with that stupid thing right now. I've got to chop ice out of the water tank." Basic chores, such as providing hay and water for the cattle sheltered in corrals, became a bitter struggle against the elements.

Today I prefer snow confined to one of those quaint decorative glass domes that I can shake on Christmas Eve when the urge for snow strikes me.

Making Music

Author at age four.

When I was four, I became obsessed with playing the piano. My contact with pianists had been limited to listening to the radio and church. The pastor's wife, who played for our services, became my role model. I loved to listen to her play hymns and was happiest when I could watch her fingers. We attended the Bethany Lutheran Church that my maternal grandfather, Gust, helped build. Many rites and milestones occurred in that white clapboard church, including my wedding.

As a child, I pounded on the big upright piano in the church basement while my mom attended Ladies Aid meetings or volunteered in the church kitchen. Mom spent considerable time cooking and cleaning there, and whenever allowed, I used the piano to entertain myself. One of our neighbors, Mildred Hanson, had a piano in her parlor, and consented to let me play it with the French doors closed to muffle the noise.

I begged for an instrument of my own, but money was short. Someone gave me a beginner's piano book. With Mom's help I quickly learned the treble clef notes and their relationship to the keyboard photo in the book. I already knew the alphabet, but I still didn't have a way to play the notes, so I decided to make myself a piano out of cardboard. Mom helped me cut a strip and divide it with a ruler and pen into eight notes, middle C to high C including sharps and flats. I then carefully colored the black notes with a crayon so it looked like the keyboard in my book. Now I had my own piano!

I laid my cardboard masterpiece on the kitchen table and propped up the songbook behind it. I then climbed up on the wooden chair and fingered the simple songs on the cardboard using the finger numbers suggested in the songbook. I had to bring the piano to life by singing the simple songs. No problem. I loved to sing. "Twinkle, twinkle, little star ..." I impressed my folks with my perseverance in learning the songs, although they wearied of my limited repertoire. I didn't know that they quietly sought a used piano to purchase.

When I was six, they bought me a beautiful spinet piano, a mahogany Kimball that belonged to Aunt Gladys, who was moving. I was thrilled beyond words, and began taking formal piano lessons from a teacher ten miles away. In the winter, Dad often drove me to the Saturday morning lesson in his Chevy pickup. The commute time was special because I had his full attention. I continued lessons for five years, through grade school, and became proficient.

Years later I learned that my Uncle Art had loaned my parents the money to buy the piano. He loved music and encouraged my interest in it. Decades later I called him to share the good news that I had purchased a grand piano. Art, now elderly, was excited. "Really? You mean one of those long ones, with the stick?"

During my childhood, I played hymns for Uncle Art. He sang tenor, Mom sang alto, and I played and sang the melody, struggling to hold my pitch against their harmonies. It began a lifelong love of choral singing.

I was fascinated by an elderly neighbor's elaborately carved pump organ. Mrs. Haugen asked me to play and sing hymns from her tattered Norwegian hymnal. She often requested her favorite, a patriotic hymn from her homeland, *Kan Du Glemme Gamle Norge.* A loose translation would be, "How Can You Ever Forget Old Norway?" My mother and my uncle, Gust Stenberg, had taught the Norwegian song to me phonetically.

"Will you play and sing for me?"

"Sure," I said, eager to get my hands on her organ. She used an old-fashioned coal cook stove and a spinning wheel, but I was most interested in the organ. I also enjoyed her freshly baked goodies.

Severely stooped and silver-haired, Mrs. Haugen listened with a faraway gaze, mouthing the words. Her weathered hands laid down her needlework as she gave the music her rapt attention. I realized the power of music when that song of her homeland evoked such strong emotions. Tears filled her pale blue eyes. Already advanced in years, she knew she'd never lay eyes on the rugged beauty of her homeland again. She lived to be ninety-six.

When I was six or seven years old, I fearlessly sang the song from memory at a fiftieth wedding anniversary celebrated at church. The Martin Bergs, the guests of honor, were Grandpa Shirley's longtime friends. We'd kept the Norwegian song a secret from grandpa. I watched his reaction as I sang, and he looked surprised. I could tell he was proud. He never complimented me, but I could tell. He smiled and asked, "How did you know the words?"

I touched a nerve with Mrs. Haugen and other Norwegian guests and received applause. The guest of honor, smiling, publicly thanked me. Then a tall man in the crowd handed me a shiny silver dollar. I was thrilled with my first—and I believe my last—paid singing gig. Mom sighed, "I wish my mother could have been alive to hear you sing that. She would have loved it." Two years later I repeated the solo for the William Jensens at their golden wedding celebration.

By age ten or eleven, I was asked to play piano for Sunday School. At first I felt honored, but later began to feel burdened after long hours each Saturday rehearsing for the Christmas program.

Beginning in junior high, I enjoyed playing the Hammond organ for church services. This provided me considerable recognition. However, it also meant time-consuming obligations with services and rehearsals. When I declined a request to play, I heard the "Don't hide your talents under a bushel" lecture, referring to the scripture passage in Matthew 5:15. Although adults meant well, they caused me guilt trips.

My parents supported me. They did not allow me to play for funerals and special services during school hours. Still, I felt considerable pressure from the community to play for church and school events while I was preoccupied with high school activities.

I was expected to volunteer my talents. I received only one dollar per Sunday service, which was not enough to buy the music I used prior to services or during the offering. I used my spending money to buy sheet music, rather than phonograph records of the latest hits such as the "Twist" by Chubby Checker or a Beach Boys tune.

In high school and college I found my niche and sang in a chorus, instead of accompanying on the piano. Making music remains a major part of my life, both playing piano for my own pleasure and singing.

Animals on the Farm

We were taught kindness to animals. My folks did not tolerate abuse or neglect of our pets or farm animals. We knew they depended on us.

I took for granted being surrounded by birds and wildlife. I didn't realize it was unusual to have our own resident bald eagle. We lived with various types of animals on the farm: work animals, such as horses; useful pets, like the German Shepherd dog who herded our cattle; breeding stock, usually huge Angus bulls; and food providers—animals raised for their meat, milk, or eggs. Sometimes the categories blurred.

Each year Dad raised calves and hogs for market, usually retaining one calf and pig to fatten for home butchering. Dad, having grown up around animals, was aware of the pitfalls of raising animals around young children. "Now, don't get attached to that pig," he'd say. "She's going to be our dinner one day."

My younger brother ignored the warnings and played with one particular pig destined for our freezer. He named her Rosebud. Big mistake. An intelligent animal, Rosebud came when called and rolled over on her back in hopes of getting her tummy scratched. Dale would release her from her pen and the hefty, pinkish pig with black markings would follow my brother.

When the pig reached maturity, Dad faced a dilemma. Rosebud ate constantly, and he couldn't afford to keep her as a pet. She took up a valuable pen in the barn, but had no additional purpose on the farm. Even the cats "earned their keep," as Dad used to say, by controlling the population of mice and gophers.

Dad could relate to our feelings for Rosebud, and he realized it would be painful for us kids if he butchered her for the family. We needed meat for winter, although we had offered to give up meat, our protein mainstay.

Dad came through with a savvy plan. He traded her to a neighbor for one of their pigs and butchered that nameless, unknown pig. We cried when our doomed pet was trucked away, but didn't have to grieve over her on a daily basis. Dale and I made a pact: we'd never eat meat of any kind when visiting that neighbor, just in case.

None of us befriended the 1500-pound Angus bulls Dad maintained. Although the breed had no horns to gore us, Dad taught us to keep our distance. I felt downright fearful of them, aware they could stomp and kill me in an instant. Whenever Dad brought home a new bull purchased from the cattle auction, we'd perch on the wooden corrals and watch the newcomer fight for dominance.

Dad picked a hot, sultry day to turn the bulls loose together from separate pens. They'd tire quickly in the heat, hopefully before they hurt each other. If one broke a leg, for example, Dad's considerable investment would have been wasted. Meanwhile, we slurped cherry Kool-Aid and gobbled chocolate chip cookies while we cheered on our particular favorite, watching the opponents roar and butt heads. Dad occasionally had to separate the aggressive animals with a sharp crack of the long rawhide bullwhip if the fight escalated. They normally established a pecking order rather quickly and tolerated each other thereafter.

We always raised chickens, replenishing the flock each year with baby chicks ordered through the mail. The just-hatched chicks arrived in special lidded cardboard boxes with air holes, twenty-five cute chicks per box, noisily chirping. We turned them loose in an area of the henhouse where we'd set up a brooder, which was a metal canopy with special light bulbs for added heat. We supplied them ground mash to eat and provided inverted glass-jar water fountains with attached saucers, designed so the chicks couldn't fall in and drown while sipping water.

One spring the chicks arrived during a late snowstorm. Mom said it was too cold to put them in the henhouse, so we kept them in our house for a couple days. During the second night one energetic male chick, bigger than the rest and already growing telltale rooster tail feathers, pecked a hole in the cardboard box, tearing an escape hole through the top. Evidently as he squeezed his body out the hole, the cover must have lifted. He set free the entire box of chicks to explore the farmhouse.

Our parents woke to a chirping mass of chicks loose in the kitchen. The chicks skittered and slid over the slick linoleum floor, some creating little puddles and piles as they explored. More than a little upset, Mom woke us up, yelling, "Hey you kids, I need help down here right now. The chicks are loose!"

Still in our pajamas, we chased down and cornered every chirping chick. We deposited each one in a tall bucket that we hauled out to the henhouse.

We found chicks hiding everywhere, inside our snow boots, behind the broom, under the appliances. The obvious ringleader seemed proud of himself, standing in a ray of sunshine and chirping louder than the rest. Once we removed the fowl to their henhouse, the real spring cleanup began on the kitchen floor, first with rags, then with a mop and hot soapy water.

◆   ◆   ◆

Of all our farm animals, our horses displayed the most intelligence. Gypsy, a cross between two breeds, a quarter horse and a Morgan, remained Dad's favorite. Gypsy was born on the farm when my father was a teenager. He trained her and took great pleasure in her graceful lines, proud carriage, and healthy dapple-gray coat. Gypsy had a natural talent for working cattle. She instinctively knew how to quickly isolate (or "cut") a calf from the rest of the herd.

In her second decade, her gray coat turned silver-white and all but the darkest spots faded. Kind in temperament, her eyes never lost their sparkle of affection for her family. Spirited whenever my father clambered up, Gypsy would actually stop and calmly wait for mom or us kids to climb up onto her back. The beautiful mare had an unusual talent. She could untie any knot with her teeth, given enough time. Dad avoided securing her with a rope, but instead attached her halter to the wooden stall with a metal chain.

Gypsy knew her daily routine. A family member rode her a mile out to pasture about the same time each evening and herded the dairy cows back towards the barn for milking. One day we had medical appointments in the city and returned home two hours past milking time. As we drove up to the farm we saw Gypsy, who'd been left in the pasture, nudging the cattle forward, gently herding them to the barn on her own. Seems she didn't need a rider after all.

Eventually an aging Gypsy had to be retired to pasture. Tears welled up in Dad's eyes when his favorite horse died at age thirty-four. When a friend asked why he never bred Gypsy, Dad replied, "She was such a beautiful horse, I didn't want her to lose her figure." Mom gasped and nearly smacked him, pointing out that she carried their three babies. My father never did live down that remark.

Next, Dad purchased a beautiful black horse named Apache, part Arabian and part quarter horse, to work the cattle. She had three white stockings and a white face. Apache's previous owner had proudly displayed a pile of ribbons and trophies that Apache had earned at horse shows, but our father wasn't interested in continuing her show business career. "Dad, why can't we enter Apache in a horse show?" we asked. "We know she'd win."

"Takes too much time to train and groom her for a show," came his usual answer. "I've got a farm. Got to put food on the table." However, he relented and let Dale show her, and Apache continued to win prizes.

Horses presented joys and dangers to us kids. When I was in grade school, a two-year-old Shetland pony arrived at our farm for boarding. The striking brown horse with full black mane and tail proved to be smart, but independent and stubborn with a mean temperament. Muscular and compact, Perky stood only thirty-six inches tall. Adults couldn't sit on him without their feet dragging the ground. "I'm too heavy for him," Dad said.

The Shetland grudgingly obeyed Dad as he fed him, but would bite and kick the rest of us with little provocation. We constantly watched for Perky's unpredictable moods. If his ears flattened, watch out. On days when Perky felt like transporting us kids around the farm, life was sweet. We'd explore the fields and pastures at will. However, when the horse got tired or lazy, he simply dumped us off and galloped home, forcing us to walk. Fortunately, we never broke any bones in the falls.

The Shetland would distend his belly as we saddled him so we couldn't get the cinch pulled tight. Later, after we'd settled in and relaxed in the saddle, he'd break into a full gallop and then suddenly stop, planting all four hooves. Invariably, we flew forward over his narrow, sloping shoulders, saddle and all, and crashed to the ground. Before we could dust ourselves off and evaluate our scrapes and bruises, he headed full-tilt for the barn, fast enough to outrun our full-size horses. If we rode him bareback, with only his mane to hang onto, we had even less chance of remaining on his back once he decided our ride had ended. Yelling at him or hitting him proved a waste of time; he simply ignored us.

A competition quickly developed between my brothers as to who could stay on Perky the longest. I refused to participate. I found his uncertain moods utterly frustrating, and gave up riding him. The pain of bruised hands and knees left me sputtering. I personally didn't care if I ever saw him again.

Word traveled about the tough little horse, and certain macho boys from the neighborhood like my cousin, Norman, tested their luck and skill. We warned them they'd be riding at their own risk, but that just encouraged them to establish their reputation, like a tough cowboy in a black-and-white western.

Perky sensed their purpose, and didn't disappoint. An experienced rider couldn't remain astride the little horse once Perky decided to dump him. If nothing else worked, Perky scraped them off his back by running close to a building. The fallen cowboys all returned to the farmyard on foot, their pride suffering the most.

After two years, we finally gave up trying to train the incorrigible horse. We sent Perky back to my uncle, who sold him. From all reports, he lived three more decades. Perky was the most ornery horse I'd ever known, the polar opposite of Gypsy.

Price family growing up on the farm. Top right: Cousins Mark and Terry with Dennis. Perky behaving for a change.

Finding Fear

I vividly recall a rare family vacation the summer I'd turned five.

"Can we go swimming now?" I asked. We impatiently waited for Mom to finish the dishes. But then our baby brother, Dale, needed a nap, so Dennis and I had to wait until he fell asleep. Finally Mom donned the new yellow print swimsuit that she had ordered from Sears especially for this Minnesota trip. She hadn't gotten it wet yet—well, at least not in the lake.

The week before the trip, when the mail order parcel arrived, Mom tried on the colorful swimsuit and went outside to model it for Dad. With a twinkle in his eye, he grabbed a nearby pail of water and announced he would "christen" it. She ran screaming toward the safety of the house.

"Keep the door closed," Dad yelled to me while laughing and chasing her across the yard. I was forced to instantly choose sides. I sided with Mom, and opened the screen door allowing her to escape back inside the house only slightly wet. Meanwhile, Dad filled a pail with icy cold water from the pump, daring her to come outdoors again.

Our family rarely spent time around lakes or rivers. Dad thought that Mom acted with extravagance when she bought a swimsuit, but didn't swim. He'd never owned a swimsuit or even rolled up his pants legs to go wading, at least that I'd witnessed. He seemed uncomfortable around water, and I remember him reading us news stories of people drowning. Then our eight-year-old cousin, Patty, drowned in a river, the first child I'd known who died. While I struggled to understand her absence, the adults in my family became paranoid around water.

Our family and Grandpa Gust had arrived at the Minnesota fishing lake after a long car trip. We were excited to stay in a little lakeside cabin. The next morning, Dad and Grandpa left early to fish in a rented boat. Dennis and I played near the frame cabin, exploring the wooded area and watching kids swim. Swimming looked easy in the calm lake. Lakes didn't move like rivers, so I wasn't afraid. I bragged that I'd know how to swim before the day ended.

Finally Mom was available to chaperone us. We entered the lake with her anxiously watching while she waded near the water's edge. We grew braver, chasing and splashing each other. What fun on a hot summer day!

Mom decided to check on my baby brother, napping a few yards away in the cabin. We weren't ready to quit, so she asked another mother on shore to keep an eye on us for a few minutes. I vaguely remember Mom's parting words, "I'll be right back. Be careful so you don't drown."

"I can go out farther than you can," Dennis taunted me as we played on the edge of the wooded lake. I recall that foliage grew right into the water without much sandy beach.

"Oh, no you can't!" I retorted, accepting his challenge like a typical five-year-old. I should have realized I stood shorter than my older brother.

"Just watch me," he goaded.

"Ready, set, go."

Fearless in my red swimsuit, I held my own, moving farther and farther into the lake just ahead of Dennis. Suddenly I tripped on undergrowth and fell face down. The cold water swept over me. My feet tangled in something and I struggled in vain, flailing. I gulped water. Everything went pitch black....

My next recollection is pain. A lady hovered over me while I was lying on the dock. I remember gasping and coughing up water. My chest felt like it would explode, and it hurt to breathe. My eyes and nose stung. My head pounded.

The tall, blonde lady Mom had asked to watch us apparently saw me go underwater and dashed in after me. I was told she carried me back to the dock and began artificial respiration. Dennis, sobbing, ran to get our mother.

Mom arrived visibly shaken, her worst fear nearly coming true. "I was only gone for a couple minutes to check the baby. What on earth happened?" She turned to the Good Samaritan. "Thank God you were here. How can I ever thank you?" My mother was so relieved I survived, she wasn't angry.

That ended my swimming debut at the lake. I quickly recovered, but didn't learn to swim that day or anytime soon. Instead, I developed a terror of drowning. The vivid memory haunted me for years, keeping me near shallow waters. I finally learned to swim a little in college, after summoning up courage to take lessons. Now I realize my limitations. I understand winning a bet is not worth losing one's life for, no matter one's age.

First Day of School

I looked up at the three-story brick schoolhouse, anchored at the end of the gravel parking lot. It cast a long shadow over the clumpy grass softball diamond and the familiar metal swing set.

Judy and Dennis ready for school.

My eight-year-old brother grabbed my hand and hurried me up the concrete steps, through the heavy double doors, past the hallway clock, and into the spotless classroom. I felt special in my twirly yellow skirt and stiff new shoes, clutching my box of Crayolas. I could smell Murphy's wax as I squeaked along the freshly shined wood floors.

I wondered what my new teacher would be like. I spotted the huge teacher's desk in the front of the room with her brass bell perched near the edge. I could hardly wait to show the teacher that I already knew how to print my name in big capital letters: J-U-D-Y. My brother took me to meet her. She must be old, I thought. She was wrinkled, gray-haired and wore a gray-flowered dress and heavy grandma shoes. "This is my sister. She's just starting first grade."

The teacher gave me a thin smile, "What's your name?"

"Judy."

"That's not a real name. Your name must be Judith." She folded her arms tightly across her ample bosom.

"No," I protested. Mommy told me. "My name is Judy."

"Judy is just a nickname. Now, Judith, go find a seat by the window."

I knew she was wrong but there was no use arguing. I'd get Mommy to tell her, I thought. This isn't what I expected. Teachers were supposed to be smart. Why didn't Miss Porter know Judy was a real name? She called my friends (Betty, Danny, and Wally) funny names, too.

Looking around from where my desk sat, I saw an American flag, which provided a splash of color in the far corner of the beige room. A painting of George Washington gazed down at us.

The rest of the morning flew by as over thirty kids tried to settle into their new school routine. The classroom held grades one through four. It was such fun to have playmates around that I started to giggle. I had known most of them before school started. I tried to remember not to hum, because my brother told me I wasn't supposed to make noise at school.

I received my very own Dick and Jane book, but I could already read it. I drew pictures in a Puzzle Pages workbook and copied the cursive letters "A" and "B" in the clean pages of my blue penmanship book, just like teacher told us. I was surprised when teacher told Darrell and Owen, "Hold your pencil in your right hand." Everybody knew they were lefties. They complained, but she didn't care.

A loud bell rang announcing lunchtime. I brought my shining blue lunch pail to my desk, like the other kids did, but was too excited to eat. When the second bell rang, allowing us to go outside to the playground, I still hadn't gotten the cap off my thermos. I didn't like milk much anyway and quickly realized no adults were around to make me drink it. I took a couple of bites from my sandwich then grabbed my chocolate chip cookie and followed the crowd.

After lunch Miss Porter told the younger students. "Now you color quietly while I start math and social studies classes with the third and fourth grades."

By three-thirty in the afternoon, her wire rim bifocals were sliding way down her nose and she wasn't smiling at all. Kids were laughing and whispering. When some boys got out of their seats, the teacher got mad. It turned out Miss Porter had a loud, scary voice. "Quiet. If you don't sit down, you'll be sorry." I felt a little knot grow in the bottom of my tummy.

She expected us to sit quietly (a tall order for first-time students) while she taught each grade separately. Whenever things dropped onto the floor, such as crayons, rulers, or personal items, Miss Porter confiscated them, locking them up in a big cabinet, never to be seen until the end of the term.

Somehow Miss Porter did not kill my enthusiasm for school. I tried so hard to please the harsh, short-tempered woman, but it was hopeless. I was social and noisy. Working in silence proved a big adjustment, especially with the excitement of having other kids around. When "playing school" at home by myself, I was accustomed to singing along with the radio's popular songs or singing with my mother who was cooking nearby. In school I upset my teacher by singing and humming while I colored. Miss Porter hated humming.

One day a few months into the term, Miss Porter told us to be quiet. Enthralled with a replacement box of Crayola crayons, I didn't know I was humming while I colored at my desk. Suddenly, after the initial warning, she flung a heavy textbook in my direction. The innocent boy next to me was struck in the throat. He was not injured, although it certainly must have been painful. I finally realized the book had been thrown at me.

I became terrified of what Miss Porter might do next if I messed up. Fear of her kept my stomach tied up in knots and made me physically ill. The humming stopped. My doctor finally counseled that I stay home one day each week to keep my digestive system on track. Lonely, I missed my classmates on Wednesdays, but I survived the term.

The school board did not extend Miss Porter's contract, so second grade became a much happier place.

What Do You Mean, We're Moving?

Arriving home from grade school one day, age nine, I spotted my piano loaded in the Chevy pickup.

"What's my piano doing in the truck?" I demanded.

"We're moving," my mother said.

I was stunned. "Today? Where?"

"Yeah, just get in the pickup. They're ready to roll." So began the great adventure.

We discovered we weren't leaving the land my grandfather farmed. We would say goodbye to a house, but not the family farm. We didn't know it, but my folks had just bought another large farm three miles away where my good friend, Iris, lived. This additional 480 acres of land came complete with a barn, granary, chicken coop, and an old house where we would immediately take up residence. My folks sold our original little house on the prairie to an elderly couple, contingent on their relocating it right away. We quickly removed our household possessions.

A few days later when we returned from school, the house was gone, as if by magic. We were disappointed we didn't see it hauled away. All that remained was the cellar pit, not so scary when exposed to sunlight.

Our parents never discussed money or financial plans with us. With gossip a well-honed pursuit in the community, their secrecy seemed motivated by a fear of us blabbing to the neighbors. It annoyed me that they didn't trust us to keep quiet. We didn't learn about most decisions until the last minute.

To expand their cropland to raise more wheat, my folks had taken out a loan to purchase the additional farmland. Dad's land transaction fit the typical pattern of farm expansion of the post-World War II period: consolidating original 160-acre homesteads into larger, more viable units.

With the transition from horses to tractors, a single farmer could farm more acres. Farms grew and Dad felt he had to expand to stay competitive. The bigger, more expensive machinery also increased expenses.

Sebastian Englerth, an early pioneer retired to town, originally owned part of the land Dad purchased. Mr. Englerth constructed the buildings himself in 1918, before farmhouses had plumbing, indoor bathrooms, or central heating. The family hosted frequent parties and dances, because the farmer-carpenter also served as a square-dance caller. They simply moved the furniture to the walls and used the open space to dance. Three neighbors, including a fiddler, provided the music.

The two-story house no doubt looked quite impressive when it was built. It had a large eat-in kitchen built so a hand pump drew water from a cistern directly into the kitchen sink. The first floor also featured a small living room with a potbellied coal stove and bedroom. The upstairs consisted of a hallway and three bedrooms, one leading to an upper-story balcony. Some rooms were warmed via a metal floor grate as the heated air drifted upward, which we later discovered provided an opportunity for eavesdropping.

The white frame home boasted a once-fashionable stained glass window panel with colorful lead glass forming a vine motif. Although structurally sound, the house had fallen into disrepair and required extensive remodeling. Even the rotting wooden balcony, packed with snow each winter, had to be removed.

Mom must have been heartbroken when she settled for that fixer-upper house, relinquishing her dream of a new home. She and Dad had planned to build one; Dad had even purchased the bulk of the lumber needed. When the land came up for sale, they only had enough money for land or a new house. Land took priority over a modern home. The lumber was eventually used to build additional corrals.

Our family of five had seriously outgrown our original one-bedroom house. The big old home, more than doubling our living space, meant three kids no longer slept on sofa beds.

"Judy, now you'll get your own bedroom," Mom said, softening the shock of losing the only house I'd known. Tiny, it would be all mine. The two boys shared the biggest bedroom, reserving the third upstairs bedroom for a hired farm hand.

Dad sold the newly acquired barn and kept the remaining buildings for grain storage. Only the house would be transported back to our original Price farm once a basement was dug for it. Dad didn't seriously consider relocating his family permanently. In addition to the sentimental family ties to his father's farm, he had made improvements, added corrals, granaries, and a two-car garage. Also, the new location added to the commute between school and town, mostly unimproved dirt roads impassable by car much of the year.

Back at school, my friend, Iris, whose family happened to be the current tenants farming the land that Dad had purchased, blamed me because she had to move out of the community. Blindsided by events, she was unprepared for changing schools or for moving to a town where her father found employment. Her folks apparently didn't prepare her or explain the economic realities to her.

"It's all your fault," Iris stammered while we were at recess. Her dark eyes flashed. "I have to move. Your folks are taking my house away," she said, using grammar-school logic. Taken aback, I was caught by surprise when she lunged at me, catching my metal hair barrette with her fingers and gouging a deep gash down my cheek. She laughed at the oozing blood and tears while I ran off to the bathroom to clean up. Although it didn't require stitches, the physical scar remained noticeable for years. I felt a deep sadness that I lost a good friend. That emotional wound hurt considerably longer.

Throughout the summer, frantic preparations prevailed at both locations. Our family spent three months living offsite in the newly purchased house while a crew dug a basement on our original farm. They chose a knoll that allowed them to tap into a shallow vein of water to pipe into the basement. We'd have hot and cold running water, forced air heating, and a basement bathroom for the first time. No more carrying water, coal, and kitchen wastes in and out every day.

Uncle Ed built the basement, as well as poured the cement floor. He stayed with our family to get the job finished. I loved watching him, an experienced mason, deftly glide the trowels back and forth to smooth and level the wet cement floor. Uncle Art completed the electrical work. Dad buried a septic tank, installed a coal forced-air furnace, and lowered our food freezer into the open basement with his hay loader.

Meanwhile, Mom worked on the interior walls of the bigger house, scrubbing off the old style calcimine, a water-based wash containing zinc oxide, glue, and coloring. She repainted with oil-based paint. She next stripped the dark varnished doors and window frames and painted them to match the walls in the style of the fifties. Each day I helped Mom set up and clean up the day's painting project. I also assisted with gardening, meals, laundry, and cleaning. I soon tired of living in the midst of dust and smelly paint thinner. The chaos continued for months while they installed new flooring and kitchen cabinetry.

One day my folks drove the grain truck to Fargo and returned laden with mismatched furniture from the secondhand store. They assigned various pieces to our bedrooms. I instantly disliked the aqua chest and a dark mahogany straight chair with red leather seat. "Oh, Mom, they're old and ugly."

"We'll just make do for a while," my mother assured me, "We'll get nicer stuff later. Have you picked out your bedspread?"

"I can't decide," I said, flipping the well-worn Sears catalog.

"We're getting a Davy Crockett bedspread," brother Dale announced, proudly modeling his coonskin cap.

I chose a white chenille bedspread with blue wedding-ring pattern trim that brightened my room. I grudgingly accepted the furniture. We never upgraded.

Eventually the house-moving day approached. A truck pulling wheeled timbers arrived to transport the newly acquired house back to our original farm where it would slide over the just completed basement. Dad planned to turn the house ninety degrees from the direction it faced on the Englerth farm, so the kitchen window faced our barn after the move. "Dad, how do you know the basement will be the right size?" I asked.

"Because we measured it," he replied, not appreciating my question.

Dad paced, periodically adjusting his seed-company cap while Mom flitted back and forth securing items in the house. My brothers and I watched with keen interest as one crew jacked up the house from its concrete perimeter foundation while another moving crew began a similar task on the barn. The buildings perched on jacks that looked like fat tinker toys. The buildings would remain elevated overnight before being rolled onto the timbers.

That evening, as we prepared for bed, deafening peals of thunder announced a fierce summer rainstorm. Our family fled from the house and spent most of a scary night in the car. Dad parked it far away from the house and barn as tornado-like winds whipped up and under the buildings, balanced precariously above the ground on the jacks. The wind howled, often shifting directions.

My brother Dennis counted the seconds between each flash of the lightning and the crack of thunder. "1001, 1002—" Then the deluge arrived. "Hey, it's raining cats and dogs."

"Let's hope this damn wind dies down soon," Dad said anxiously puffing his Camel cigarette and peering into the darkness. "I'm afraid it's powerful enough to lift that house off the jacks," he said shaking his head. Each time a jagged lightning bolt lit up the night sky, we confirmed that the house remained intact.

Thankfully, we escaped a catastrophe, and after a few hours the wind gusts abated. The rain slowed to a steady downpour, and we returned to the house for fitful sleep. We awoke the next morning to a blue sky with fluffy clouds. Both crews arrived early, but the saturated dirt road presented a new complication for them. Would it support the weight of the heavy load? One worker asked the question out loud, "What are we going to do if one of the moving rigs gets stuck in the road?" They shook their heads, but remained silent.

In the end all went smoothly, and everyone breathed a sign of relief. We wanted to ride in the house as it moved down the road, but Dad nixed that idea. No use pressing our luck more than we already had.

Gardening

We learned the cycles of farming and its unpredictable nature from our family garden. We grew juicy tomatoes, lettuce, and onions to eat fresh. Mom raised carrots, green beans, and cucumbers for preserving. Some years we harvested bountiful squash and pumpkins. Dad planted long rows of potatoes and sweet corn in a nearby field. Mom canned the produce, including corn, in glass Mason jars. We dug up potatoes by hand in the fall and stored them in our root cellar (later in our new basement) for winter eating.

Ready for Halloween.

In the spring, Dad cultivated the soil in the garden plot with his tractor and plow, adding aged barnyard fertilizer. The rest of the garden's care rested squarely with my mother and us kids. We each planted a small area of our own with seeds Mom provided. I preferred onions because the bulbs popped up in a few days, giving me instant satisfaction.

Weeding and watering the garden consumed countless hours from May until September, especially on years with scanty rainfall. Rain was always unpredictable. Our short growing season limited us, and sometimes we covered the ripening produce with blankets or tarps to protect it from an early frost. Other years hail or grasshoppers would shred our entire efforts.

With such odds, we learned no one could guarantee a harvest each year. On a small scale, we learned the volatility of farming. If our cucumbers froze prematurely, we went without pickles. However, if Dad's wheat crop failed, the family had to survive on less income for a whole year, and he probably had to take on debt.

Peas were my favorite. As a preschooler I believed I had successfully "stolen" fresh peas from the vine. I didn't realize that I'd left an incriminating trail of empty pods. Mom didn't mind; at least I was eating healthy. Remembering how sweet those fresh peas tasted still makes me grin. Tomatoes were a different story. My brothers and I got scolded if we plucked tomatoes prematurely. Once we got into real trouble when we pulled up a whole row of tiny carrots looking for two big enough to snack on.

Fencing kept the bigger wild critters out of the garden, but we lost plants to pocket gophers that ate certain roots. Eventually, we found a cat that caught gophers when they popped up from their underground burrows. She'd sit by their hole for hours, silently waiting, then grab the doomed rodent by the throat. Her kittens learned the same skill, so they were in big demand by our neighbors.

My older brother set out metal spring-loaded traps to kill mice and gophers, until my little brother accidentally caught his fingers in one. I arrived just after it happened, but wasn't strong enough to release the trap. I ran yelling and waving my arms to alert Dad who was driving the tractor nearby. He jumped off, ran to the screaming toddler, and opened the trap, releasing his fingers. Somehow Dale escaped serious injury.

Our garden was located near its water source, our windmill, complete with an electric pump and wooden tank to hold water for the livestock. We used a rubber hose to divert fresh water from the pump to the garden rows. The round tank measured ten feet across with two feet of water in it. Dad sometimes dumped minnows in it to clean up summer algae.

One hot August day while Dennis and I, aged seven and five, had been instructed to water the garden, Dennis got bored and decided he'd rather fish for the little minnows. I helped him slide a long plank of lumber across the top of the tank. He brought out his new fishing pole complete with line and hook and climbed out on the plank.

"Look at me," he bragged. "I'm gonna catch those fish." Before I could even beg for a turn at the fishing pole, I heard a splash. He had fallen off the narrow board into the water, clothes and all. At least he was barefoot. I stared wide-eyed as he scrambled up and climbed out, dripping wet with moss in his hair, just his ego bruised.

He looked so funny I laughed. All the commotion alerted my mother, who arrived to end his fishing stint. She didn't think it was funny. "Don't you ever do that again, young man!" she admonished him as she swatted him on the bottom and marched him to the house for cleanup. "You could've drowned."

I recall another day in the garden years later. I'd turned on the hose at a slow trickle to water the tomatoes, and then took a detour to check out the new kitten. He was asleep, all curled up in a furry white ball. The mother cat, spotting me near her newborn, quickly arrived. The kitten began to nurse contentedly.

"You know I'm not going to take your kitten," I assured the proud calico mother. Petting her gently, I told Princess, "Your baby is so cute." She purred loudly and nuzzled my hand as if she understood every word.

"Now Princess, what should I name him?" I'd used so many names through the years, I ran out of unique ones. I couldn't use Snowball again and again.

Returning to my garden chores, I noticed the green beans appeared ripe. I hoped Mom didn't decide to can this afternoon. I wanted some time off to read.

Dad assigned each of us a few acres of barley. The proceeds of those harvests became our primary allowance for the year. We purchased a savings bond with the income. It taught us to be junior farmers.

One year we had ample rainfall and grew a bumper crop of sweet corn. We kids harvested it (hot, heavy work) and sold it in Robinson, door to door, out of our pickup, with Mom driving. Selling it for a penny a cob, plus tips, we earned enough money to buy our first bicycle for thirty-plus dollars. The three of us planned to share it. Much to my chagrin, I got outvoted. We purchased a boy's bike.

One of Dad's goals was to raise us to be moral people instilled with a work ethic. Growing our own food became part of that training. "I want you to know the value of a dollar," was one of his favorite sayings as we labored in the fields and gardens or weeded the trees. I believe we learned that lesson.

When Do We Eat?

Food played a central role in the lives of my parents and grandparents as they struggled on the prairie of the upper Midwest. They planted, tended, harvested, preserved, and prepared food daily. They raised food to sustain themselves, and sold grain and animal products, particularly eggs and cream, to buy what they couldn't grow. My grandparents purchased salt and spices, sugar, molasses, coffee, and cocoa. Because North Dakota's growing season is too short for most fruits, my family bought peaches and cherries in large quantities for canning.

Our men took great pride in feeding their families. I heard both Grandpa Gust and my father express gratitude that they had never gone to bed hungry, as so many others did, during the Great Depression. However, the threat of hunger impacted them. "Clean up your plate. Many kids in the world are starving," Dad used to say. My folks were charter members of the Clean Plate Club. If we dawdled, we were reminded of the less fortunate.

If any food was rationed when I was young, it was ready-to-eat, purchased foods such as potato chips, candy bars, and "pop," as we called carbonated beverages. I still hear Mom's admonition, "Hey, take it easy on that catsup. That isn't cheap." Hamburger meat, because we raised it, was unlimited.

Mom's sisters told of how they divided an egg for breakfast in lean times and packed home-baked slices of bread smeared with homemade syrup for their school lunches. A generation later, my brothers and I carried bologna, egg, or roast beef sandwiches with cookies or brownies. Nothing was wasted in either generation.

In the days before anyone understood cholesterol's role in cardiovascular health, "eating well" meant unending animal products.

Males in the family supplemented the beef, pork, and chicken they produced on the farm by hunting pheasants and prairie chicken. In the fall, they hunted deer as well as migrating ducks and geese, adding variety to our meals. Learning to hunt was a rite of passage for the boys, almost like joining a fraternity or brotherhood. The gun culture continues yet today. The women didn't have a comparable activity, although a few females hunted, and most helped dress the wild game and cook it.

Cooking involved time-consuming, difficult labor. Farmers ate three hot meals each day—breakfast, dinner, and supper, plus mid-afternoon lunches and snacks. No fast food or frozen entrees existed. For the first half of the twentieth century, meals in my family were cooked from scratch without the help of hot running water, refrigerators or iceboxes, and electricity. Mom used a bottled-gas kitchen range and oven instead of a coal cook stove, but otherwise prepared meals much the same as her mother and grandmother had done until electricity belatedly arrived on our farm. Rural gender roles remained rigid; food preparation fell squarely into the woman's domain. Men only cooked when no women lived in the home, such as before Dad married. He was thrilled to relinquish that task.

School-age children on the farm played a major role in raising food. Each family member performed daily tasks assigned based on strength, age, and sex. Kids provided considerable labor for the summer vegetable gardens as well as the sweet corn and potato fields. We all worked hard.

During the grammar school years, my brothers and I helped care for the poultry and farm animals and milked the cows. Mom or I washed the messy cream separator every day. Mom usually plucked and gutted the farm-raised chickens, a job I detested. Dennis and Dale each graduated from helping Mom in the henhouse and garden to more valued men's work, revolving around crops and beef cattle, work requiring considerable physical strength. In a pinch the women assisted with men's work, never the other way around. As the only daughter, I remained the cooking assistant and chief bottle-washer.

We gathered with relatives on holidays, usually Pearl and Emil, and their children, Dianne and Tom, alternating between homes. We usually included Uncle Art, Uncle Ed, and Grandpa Shirley, all older, single men who loved a home-cooked meal. Dad loved playing the generous host to friends, relatives, and even businessmen coming to the farm. With a sweep of the arm he invited everyone for meals, including the gas deliveryman, usually without notice. Mom made the stew stretch or quietly gave up her pork chop to accommodate the extra person.

Because Grandpa Gust, the widowed patriarch, lived nearby, we hosted many Shirley relatives. When visiting him, they often ate at our farm. To my eyes, some of our guests measured hospitality by the spread presented for them. As a child I loved the excitement of guests as well as the extra desserts. I looked forward to Sunday when cousins came by to play. As I grew older, I resented the hours of preparation and endless dishes.

My mother, Evelyn, baked fantastic dinner rolls and caramel rolls. It appeared to me the more our guests heaped compliments on Mom, the more she cooked and baked. City relatives went on and on, "I'll have another roll. Homemade jam and butter. Can't buy this stuff. Homegrown beef! Evelyn, how do you do it?"

Dad's response to her culinary skills was simply to pat his stomach and smile, "Fine meal, Evelyn."

♦   ♦   ♦

One summer morning, hoping to speed up the rising process of the bread dough, Mom followed through on a bright idea. She placed the pans of dough, covered by a kitchen towel, on the back window shelf of the family car. She could then bake bread before the mid-afternoon heat. It seemed like a great plan until Dad, without warning, drove off in the car. He had not noticed the bread pans in the back when he headed to town to get some hardware. Mom didn't realize the car was missing until time to punch the dough down.

"Where did Bruce go?" she asked Uncle Art, who was repairing machinery in the farmyard.

"To Tuttle for parts. If they don't have the right size, he'll go on to the next place," Art responded.

"Oh, no. My dough is going to spill over and make a sticky mess all over the car," she worried. "It won't be fit to eat, and it'll be too late to make another batch for supper." A meat and potatoes man, Dad didn't consider any meal complete without bread and butter.

Mom impatiently watched and waited for Dad's return, which took nearly three hours. "I can picture the dough rising over its pans in that hot car and oozing over the seats," she worried, wringing her hands in a kitchen towel.

Dad, preoccupied and oblivious to his cargo, pushed back his denim cap and laughed heartily as he saw Mom hurriedly rescue her six overgrown loaves. The dough hung precariously over the edges of the pans. Mom expressed relief. "Thank goodness. They're still intact, and I don't have a big mess." She quickly baked the loaves in spite of the heat. Dad couldn't resist the aroma when he came in for his afternoon coffee. Grabbing a bread knife, he sampled the end slice as he teased his wife about starting a bakery route.

Dad expected meals on the table promptly when he and the male workers arrived back in the yard at noon or at the end of the workday. In the summer that twelve-hour workday ended after seven p.m. During harvest season, the men worked even longer until dark, closer to nine p.m. When the men and boys finished eating the evening meal, they rested.

I resented women's work after supper. No matter that the men may have started earlier or worked longer hours—I felt anything but energetic in the evening. I hated doing the fourth or fifth round of dishes for the day while they relaxed. I wasn't working on my own, of course; Mom always worked beside me. When we finally finished scrubbing the greasy pots and pans, we left the hot kitchen and joined the others outside.

One August evening as the sun sank low in the crimson sky and disappeared, we headed to the front yard. As the light faded, Dad, wearing a blue chambray shirt and wide-leg denim jeans, put his newspaper down on the concrete block steps and stretched out on the grass. He'd already shed his heavy work boots. We watched lightning glow in the distance. "Someone's getting rain," he noted. "Hope it's our turn soon. Sure need it."

Soon the expansive prairie sky grew dark, and one by one the stars magically appeared.

"I see the Big Dipper," Dale said, pointing to the twinkling stars in the northern sky.

"There's the Little Dipper," Dennis added.

"When will we see the Northern Lights again?" I asked no one in particular. "We haven't seen them in a long time." No one seemed to know. Uncle Art, our hired man, tilted his balding head skyward, identifying planets and constellations.

Eventually the swarms of mosquitoes grew thick and annoying, and everyone retreated inside to go to bed. Except for the bread incident, it had been a typical summer day on our North Dakota farm. Providing bountiful food for the family was one measure of a successful family man. Using that standard, both grandfathers and my father were wildly successful.

From top. Shirley grandparents with Dennis and Judy.
Gust with grandkids in 1963 and 1951.

Pearl, Dad's sister, and her husband, Emil Janke.

Playing in hay with cousins Glenda and Sharon Shirley.
Janke and Price cousins.

Shirley siblings, 1986. Rear: Evelyn, Edna, Agnes, Hilda, Minnie, Art, Gladys, Gilma, front: Melvin, Glen, and Gilbert.
Lower photo: Shirley-Stenberg celebration 1949.

Great-Grandpa Daniel's Adventures

"Hi, kids. How was school?" asked our father as he picked us up from Robinson School in our black Hudson.

"OK," we said, almost in unison, as we tumbled into the car with jackets, papers, and lunch pails. Typically, Dennis arrived first and grabbed the front passenger seat. Dale and I shared the backseat, each claiming a window.

"What did you learn today?"

Dale held up a completed workbook page hastily colored. But his mind remained on the playground. "Made a home run today at second recess. Went way over their heads," Dale said.

"Good for you."

"I got a 100 on my spelling test," I reported.

"Good girl."

"How about you, Dennis?" Dad asked as he carefully maneuvered the car out of the busy parking lot and onto the gravel road heading the five miles back to the farm.

"We talked about the Civil War. Mr. Lane told us about the battle of the *Merrimac* and the *Monitor*, the big ironclad ships. Wasn't your grandpa on the *Monitor*?"

"You mean Daniel Price. He fought in Mobile Bay in Alabama for the Union side, but he wasn't on the *Monitor*. He sailed on a smaller ironclad ship called the *Kickapoo*. Your history book probably doesn't mention the *Kickapoo*."

"That's a funny name," I said.

"Oh, It's probably an Indian name. The ship was built after the Merrimac/Monitor battle. Daniel volunteered to join the Navy in the summer of 1864.

A few years earlier he had a timber boat on Lake Huron where he traded with the Indians in Canada."

"Real Indians, living in the wild? Neat!"

"Yes. Before white settlers took over their land for farming and cut down the trees."

"Why did your grandpa go to Canada?"

"For work. He came here from England in April, 1853. Remember, I told you, Daniel was only sixteen years old when he came with his older brother, William. He'd heard of jobs at the Northwest Fur Company.

"Did he get along with the Indians?"

"Yeah, I think so. Had a scar on his arm from when an Indian slashed him with a knife, but he didn't hold that against the rest of them. Daniel said the Indians treated him fairly when trading."

"But I thought he was a homesteader."

"Yes, later. Daniel was too young at first. Had to be twenty-one to homestead land."

"Wasn't your grandma French?" Dennis asked.

"Yes, Polly Valad. Her family was living in Bruce County, Canada, when she and Daniel met and got married. They moved to Michigan. Then Daniel left for the Civil War for two years. After the war he bought a farm in Michigan. That's where my Dad, Tom, was born. Later they moved to South Dakota to homestead. Our cousins still live there."

"How do you know that stuff?"

"Oh, my father used to talk about it. Plus we have old pictures," he said, turning off the gravel road and onto the dirt road leading to the farmstead. The time had passed quickly, while listening to Dad's stories. He made history come alive.

As Dad pulled to a stop, we scrambled. Dennis yelled, "Race you. Last one to the house is a rotten egg." Being older, he was halfway there.

◆   ◆   ◆

Dad wasn't the only storyteller in the family. Dad's sister, Pearl, teased him by telling us about incidents when he got into trouble as a kid. After she revealed one particular story to us, he decided to put his spin on it. Dad could hardly finish the tale without dissolving into laughter.

In the 1920s, oil fever wasn't lost on the area children. My father and his playmate, John, concocted a story that they had found oil in the village of Robinson. Bruce and John poured a can of motor oil they had scavenged into an abandoned hole, just to test everyone's reaction.

As the tale goes, the boys ran to tell the exciting news to my grandmother, Adria, who fell for the ruse. Adria drew the blinds in the house that she and the kids lived in during the school year while she examined the evidence. "Looks like oil. We'll have Tom check it out."

She contacted John's mother and admonished her, "Please don't say a word to anyone." The families were sworn to secrecy. With the mothers hoping it was true, the scared pranksters didn't dare own up to the deed. "Promise you won't tell," Bruce begged his friend. "We'll get in trouble."

Adria sent a note via a neighbor to her husband, Tom, on the farm directing him to come to town at once. The boys could hardly sleep. Their little white lie had snowballed and spun out of control. Then Tom arrived. After smelling and tasting the "black gold," he contacted the other boy's father. Under cover of darkness the men investigated the oil hole. Using a lantern, they soon found the discarded oilcan smeared with little fingerprints in a nearby ditch.

The embarrassed mothers roundly chastised the culprits, but somehow the boys avoided a spanking for lying. Tom didn't have the heart to punish. He could barely keep a straight face in front of the boys. The perpetrators felt relief when they were busted. They learned it was hard work promoting snake oil.

Help Thy Neighbor

"I helped save a farm today," Dad declared as he wearily slumped into the kitchen chair nearest the door. "The flames stopped right at the fire break I'd just plowed."

He'd just returned home, dirty and exhausted. Grit and charcoal blackened all exposed skin on his face, neck, and hands like cheap minstrel paint. The whites of his eyes appeared red, irritated from the blowing dirt and soot. His clothes and hair reeked of smoke. He and a group of volunteers had spent a grueling day battling a grass fire. Dad had driven his John Deere tractor to the site and plowed up the grass and cropland several yards wide around a farmstead potentially in the fire's path. It worked. Lack of fuel finally halted the approach of the voracious fire. The farm survived.

Dad frequently received requests to help in local emergencies. Neighbors were expected to lend a hand in any crisis, whether a prairie fire, an accident, or an injury. With no local emergency services available, and one sheriff for the entire 144-square-mile county, farmers and villagers became interdependent. Rural communities felt a connectedness that city dwellers didn't understand.

From the earliest years, prairie fires threatened the North Dakota farms and villages. We'd all heard stories of an out-of-control prairie fire. With few lakes and no rivers, and no major highways to stop it, a raging fire could burn a path of destruction for miles. Tall grasses and unrelenting winds fueled the rolling inferno, which consumed everything in its path. Farmers would complete a plowed firebreak only to have the wind shift and send flames rushing headlong in another direction.

◆   ◆   ◆

As a teenager, I witnessed the devastation caused by one fire. Aunt Minnie and Uncle Gust's residence (an old hotel building) in the town of Robinson caught fire one blustery October day.

I was sitting in school on that windy afternoon in 1959. Our principal, Mr. Lundberg, interrupted our class with a knock. "Need the bigger guys to help carry furniture away from a burning building," he said. Hands shot up. That sounded far more exciting that the history lesson Mr. Monilaws had scheduled. Several of the boys, including my brother Dennis, ran to the fire scene just blocks from the school. The rest of us couldn't concentrate on schoolwork. Adult volunteers had managed to snatch a few pieces of furniture and clothing from the smoldering building and haul them outdoors. The students then moved the rescued items farther away from the fire.

Dad had spotted the smoke plume rising over five miles away. He dropped his farm work and rushed to the fire scene, not knowing until he arrived it was his brother-in-law's home. Mom followed in another vehicle. When she found out whose house was on fire, she picked Dale and me up from school. We rushed to Minnie and Gust's home, by then fully engaged in flames. With only distant well water and little fire-fighting equipment available, saving the building proved futile.

As part of the growing crowd of spectators, I watched in horror as the flames hissed and crackled, consuming the two-story wood building. The upper story collapsed and the whole building slowly burned to the ground. The fire consumed my aunt's photos and possessions, leaving a heap of blackened rubble.

The thick smoke and soot stung my eyes and nose. Hot embers swirled near my hair in the chaotic air currents. "Watch those ashes. Stamp them out," someone shouted. "Don't let them start a new fire." A fire truck and volunteers eventually arrived from neighboring Pettibone. They helped save nearby homes and businesses. Luckily, no one was injured.

The village of Robinson didn't acquire a fire truck until 1962, when Robinson organized a formal volunteer fire department. In reality, these same men had been volunteering as firefighters without equipment for years. Now they had an official title and a used fire truck with a siren, financed by benefit fundraisers. Volunteers kept the truck's reservoir filled with water from a flowing well at the Whitman farm east of town.

Their most unusual fire run happened during a firemen's benefit dance. The shrill fire siren sounded over the twang of country music. "I hear the siren," one dancer yelled. "Is this for real?"

Several well-dressed men stopped in mid-step, ran next door to the firehouse, and zealously climbed aboard the old fire truck—some sober, others not. Within moments, the loaded truck pulled out. "Everybody's here. Let's roll."

Before the end of the night they'd saved a house while still in their dancing shoes. Back at the dance, the volunteers now had plenty to celebrate.

◆   ◆   ◆

Dad often helped disabled motorists. Sometimes he pulled them out of an icy ditch with a tractor and cable. Other times, his labors involved a combination of shoveling and towing a vehicle out of a snowdrift. Dad wouldn't take payment for his services, although he once accepted a Mormon Bible from a grateful missionary.

"Stop and help the next guy in trouble," he told those in need. "What goes 'round, comes 'round."

One of Dad's favorite stories, retold and often embellished, stands out in my memory. One brisk autumn weekend, Dad spent hours retrieving a Volkswagen Bug with his John Deere tractor and cable. The car had been mired in quicksand at nearby Horsehead Lake. The novice goose hunters from Bismarck walked to the farm for help. Unfamiliar with the terrain, the teenagers had driven deep into wet bogs.

Dad returned home exhausted from that particularly difficult rescue. Irritated at the trouble the young men had caused, he decided to make an exception and accept payment. He shook his head in disgust when we pressed for details. "I really lectured those two guys for doing something so stupid," he told the family. "Darn lucky they didn't lose their car." Dad recounted the story often to illustrate how the local farmers rescued the incompetent out-of-town hunters.

Some years passed. Then at his niece Shirley's wedding, Dad was being introduced to the groom, Chuck. He took a closer look at Dad and announced with a grin, "Oh, we've met. Remember the quicksand?"

"Oh no, was that you?" Dad asked laughing.

"Afraid so."

"Don't let him near that lake," Dad advised the bride.

Sure enough, Chuck had married into the family. They laughed at the irony and ended up hunting buddies, now with Dad navigating away from the quicksand.

Manhunt

Everything changed when the convicts escaped on June 24, 1973.

Up until that time, our North Dakota farmhouse had remained unlocked. Dad didn't own a house key. Vehicle keys routinely dangled from their ignitions. In the winter, we often left a parked car with its engine running while doing errands. Theft was rare in our community; farm machinery worth thousands of dollars sat unattended in the fields near highways. Most farmers simply relied on noisy guard dogs to protect their farmstead from any teenage joy riders who might be tempted to siphon gas from fuel tanks.

One Sunday evening in 1973, a stolen car, crammed with ten convicted criminals, ran out of gas near our farm. Their presence would jolt the sleepy, law-abiding countryside.

The convicts had overpowered a newly hired, unarmed prison guard, holding a sharpened table knife to his throat. They used their hostage to get three other unarmed guards to comply with their demands. Binding and gagging all four guards, the convicts had locked them in a cell and made their planned escape.

Lashing four steel beds together, one of the prisoners had climbed to the top of the North Dakota State Penitentiary walls. He attached a rope made of twisted, knotted bed sheets, which they all used to lower themselves to freedom. They then hot-wired a car near the prison grounds and gained at least one hour's lead before their escape was discovered.

The getaway car sped eastward on Interstate 94 from Bismarck and then turned north toward Canada, but they didn't make it to the border. About sixty miles into the escape, the stolen car ran out of gas, miles from any gas station. Law enforcement officials, suddenly on full alert, soon located the abandoned car, and the local manhunt began. Sheriff's officials, highway patrol officers, and local police went farm to farm spreading the word, "Be very careful. These guys could be violent. Three broke jail before. They won't want to go back."

Rumors quickly spread that the convicts were rapists and murderers. One had been serving up to fifteen years for first-degree robbery. Some of their crimes had been violent. But in reality, they hadn't murdered anyone—yet.

The authorities warned the locals, "They've been incarcerated for stealing, but you be careful. They won't hesitate to take hostages. We don't think they're armed, but we consider them dangerous. We believe they only have hammers and tools. They'll be looking for guns." This was gun country. Most farmers and villagers owned several long guns for hunting. Authorities and the general public feared the convicts would attempt to steal them. Locals secured their weapons.

The deputies knew the escapees couldn't travel far on foot on the largely treeless prairie without being seen. On Day One, authorities captured five of the fugitives, in two groups, without resistance. Five remained at large. Most farms were located one to three miles apart on unmarked gravel roads. "See anything unusual?" the deputy asked as he visited local farms.

"Nope. Everything is quiet."

By Day Two, anxieties heightened among the locals. Fear replaced trust and openness as citizens looked over their shoulders at the slightest noise. A routine dogbark evoked terror. Farmers and villagers installed locks.

The women worried that the fugitives could be lying in wait. "What if they're out there watching me?" one farm wife asked, staring into the distance. "They could grab me after the men leave for the fields."

"I'm getting out of here," declared another as she packed clothes for herself and her children and drove off to stay with relatives.

Tension mounted as Day Two came and went. People began warily watching for strangers in their midst. A farmer noticed that his dog food in an isolated storage shed had been noticeably depleted. The authorities continued to search the open fields and abandoned buildings.

Farm work continued. My father carried a loaded shotgun with him as he and my brother Dale, twenty-two, mowed and raked hay fields with their tractors. Their eyes scanned the vast horizons for unfamiliar movement as they worked. Horses, police dogs, small planes, and a helicopter joined the vehicle search over rough terrain. Volunteers and authorities probed trees, bushes, outhouses, ditches, and tall rushes—any place a man could hide. A civilian accidentally shot himself in the leg. Fear was palpable.

On Day Three, two escapees approached Vera Wetzel's secluded farmhouse on foot, wearing their nondescript, dark green work clothes and tan work shoes. They politely knocked on her locked screen door. Seeing the short, slight woman inside, one called out, "We ran out of gas just up the road. Like to use your phone."

"I don't have a phone," Vera lied, praying it wouldn't ring within their hearing. She suspected these strangers might be the fugitives.

"Maybe we could borrow your car for a little while, " said the tall one, standing over six feet with intense, dark eyes. The shorter, blue-eyed man, visibly nervous, remained silent.

"No, I don't have the keys."

"Is your husband home? Maybe he can help."

"Yes, he's in the barn." Vera answered. She wondered if they believed her. Had they been watching when her husband, Ted, left for the fields that morning?

"Who's with you? I hear someone talking."

"Oh, just the TV," she said, this time forgetting to lie and mentally kicking herself. She explained later that she regretted admitting she was alone.

As the two men walked toward the barn, Vera closed and locked both doors and raced to the phone for help. She couldn't find the sheriff's number so she made a frantic call to a neighbor. "They're here, in my yard!" Vera screamed into the phone in panic, "I'm alone. Please get me help. Quick."

"I'll call the sheriff," the neighbor said. He hung up and placed a call to the command center a few miles away. "They've been sighted at Wetzels'. She's alone. Hurry."

Meanwhile the intruders looked around the empty Wetzel barn. Finding no one, they approached Vera's car parked near the house. They were out of luck. Her husband, Ted, had removed the car keys earlier. They tried unsuccessfully to hotwire her car, but quickly abandoned the effort. They desperately needed a ticket out of the area.

Seeing them approach her house a second time from her kitchen window, Vera looked toward the road. Still no sign of help. She made a second panicked phone call. She hoped it wouldn't be her last. She dialed another neighbor's number from memory.

My mother, Evelyn, answered the call just as Dad and my brother Dale, recently discharged from the army, arrived home for their noon meal.

"They're coming back to the house, and I'm alone!" Vera screamed into the phone.

"Bruce and Dale are here. They'll help you," Mom said.

The men grabbed their deer rifles and dashed to the pickup. They raced to the pre-designated sheriff's command post, but it had been vacated. Had someone notified the authorities? Dad and Dale then sped down the lonely gravel road, two-and-a-half miles north to Vera's farm. Both were excellent marksmen; both were prepared to save their threatened neighbor.

Back at Vera's farm, the convicts had rushed into a small covered entry porch to Vera's house. They tried to break down the seldom-used front door. Miraculously, they couldn't force the solid wooden door open. Her husband hadn't trimmed the bottom when the thick new carpet was installed. For once, procrastination paid off. Vera's two dogs sensed the danger. Hearing the menacing voices and thumps against the door, they abandoned Vera and ran for cover under a bed. These same noisy dogs growled and barked menacingly whenever we had visited.

Dad and Dale, first to arrive, slowly drove into the farmyard, every sense on full alert. Quickly scanning the scene, they circled the farmyard in their pickup. Nothing seemed amiss. Then Dad spotted a pair of eyes peering out from the bottom corner of the window in the entry porch. He stopped the pickup, watched, and waited. Dad and Dale didn't know how many convicts were present, if they were armed, or even if they'd already grabbed Vera.

Back in the house, Vera cowered on the inside of the front door. Her heart pounding, she overheard the convicts discussing the men in the pickup. "What are they doing? They've got guns! I see another car coming. Somebody called."

Suddenly the fugitives bolted. The cornered men dashed outside and made a run for a nearby haystack. Adrenaline flowing, Dad and Dale jumped out of the pickup with their rifles and ordered them to stop.

"Halt. Hold it right there, or we'll shoot." The convicts continued to flee.

"Shoot above them. Don't kill them," Dad said, remembering that Dale had recent combat training.

Dad and Dale shot a dozen rounds into the air to scare them. It worked. The intruders leaped for cover, diving into the nearby haystack. They remained motionless. Silence. No one knew who'd make the next move. Dad and Dale, rifle barrels glinting in the sun, kept them trained on the hay. Empty rifle casings lay strewn at their feet.

The crack of shots helped direct the deputies who were nearby. Guns drawn, the authorities quickly joined Dad and Dale, who now lowered their guns and watched with keen anticipation.

Within fifteen minutes, nearly thirty police vehicles from various jurisdictions came screeching into the farmyard in a cloud of dust, followed by several neighbors. The uniformed deputies flanking the haystack identified themselves and called out, "You're surrounded. Give yourselves up."

Silence. Nothing stirred.

"This is the sheriff. You can't escape. Surrender immediately."

After a few moments the lawmen cautiously poked around the edges of the hay with a pitchfork. They found nothing. A late-arriving deputy wiped the sweat from his brow with his uniform sleeve. "Lady, you sure they're hiding in this hay?"

"Positive. My neighbors saw them, too," she said pointing to Dad and Dale.

"Oh, they're in there, all right," Dale said. "Two of them."

"Bring on the police dogs."

The trained dogs quickly sniffed out the two men buried deep in the haystack. The wary convicts slowly climbed out, their hair covered with hay, their hands raised. They scanned the gun-toting civilians and quickly surrendered to uniformed authorities.

Police handcuffed and searched them. Vera noticed the blisters on the convict's feet when their shoes and socks were removed. To everyone's relief, the escapees only carried razor blades. They hadn't been able to steal guns. After being placed in the police car, one of the convicts told the deputies, "I thought those crazy farmers were going to kill me."

"Yeah, you're darn lucky to be alive. These people stick up for each other," the officer said. "You're better off back in the penitentiary."

Suddenly Vera began chattering non-stop, hands gesturing, to the gathering crowd of onlookers. "I thought they had me. Boy, was I glad to see Bruce's pickup show up. That big guy could move. I've never seen anyone run so fast in my whole life."

The community's relief was tempered with the realization that three criminals remained at large. It was premature to let their guard down.

Over the next two days the remaining escapees lost hope of obtaining guns and transportation. They surrendered peacefully, one by one. They complained of hunger, although one admitted he'd survived on milk from a dairy farm. The last convict was captured fifteen miles from the abandoned car. Finally one lady had proof of theft: "John, I told you your overalls couldn't have blown off our clothesline. He's wearing them!"

The manhunt was over, but it took years for the rural community to recover its shattered sense of safety and security. Perhaps it never did. Although North Dakota normally has the lowest crime rate in the nation, a new generation felt vulnerable.

Circle of Life

Dale, Judy, Evelyn, and Dennis Price. Bruce passed away in 1990.

One hundred years after my grandparents arrived on the North Dakota prairie and broke the land to the plow, the land remains a constant. Gazing over northern Kidder County, one sees only a few visual changes from land use in 1910.

The open grazing lands of the nineteenth century buffalo (bison) era are now fenced for individual herds of beef cattle, dividing the land into squares. Pastures with grazing cattle border cultivated fields. Agriculture is still the primary economic pursuit, with crops no longer limited to grains, especially the wheat, oats, and barley crops of my grandparents' era. Irrigation equipment has arrived. Today fields of potatoes, corn, and giant sunflowers that follow the sun alternate with grain crops and grasslands.

Many acres have been idled by government incentives to take land out of production or preserve wetlands. Farmers continue to explore alternative fuels markets using abundant prairie grass or corn. Biofuels offer hope for the future.

Miles of electric poles and high-voltage transmission lines stretch over the rolling countryside. Lonely cellular phone towers reach skyward.

Deciduous trees now dot the landscape. Planted trees grow in clusters or rows around the abandoned sites of early farmsteads where an occasional leaning structure remains. The thousands of small family farms that homesteaders established throughout the county have merged into about 250 larger ones that remain economically viable. These remaining farmers plant long rows of trees called shelterbelts to protect their farms from strong wind and blowing snow.

Lonely gravel roads follow the original surveyor's section lines; paved roads connect supply towns. The railroad spurs that brought the settlers here are gone. Only one railroad line remains in the county, a freight line running through Steele and Dawson, bordering Interstate 94. The other rails have been abandoned to the network of highways that carry the people and their products to markets in the distant cities.

Creeks shifted course and lakes merged throughout the century. A higher water table created bigger lakes and more sloughs in the glacial pothole country loved by waterfowl. Horsehead Lake, within sight of our Price farm, joined Cherry Lake. The water expanded to swallow up our former pasture, rotting the wooden fence posts Dad had pounded into the sandy soil decades earlier. Even high-voltage transmission towers had to be rerouted at considerable expense to skirt the encroaching lake.

Some of the land broken to the plow and seeded to grain by my grandfathers has now come full circle. It has been converted back to grasslands and wetlands to preserve the North American central flyway and its migratory bird habitat. The wetlands, many acres formally preserved in a natural state, remain as a vital part of the nesting grounds of ducks, geese, sandhill cranes, as well as songbirds. They use the route on their annual pilgrimage, as they have for generations.

White tail deer remain plentiful, their numbers controlled by the fall hunting seasons that attract hunters from throughout America. Hunting season is high tourist season in Kidder County.

Although its 1,433 square miles of land and lakes are a mecca for deer, fowl, and small game, Kidder County's human population has dwindled to that of the earliest years of pioneer settlement, a hundred years ago. Currently, only two people per square mile live in my home county.

My grandfathers could not have envisioned the boom and bust cycles ahead as they gazed over their homesteads. They saw a land of milk and honey, ripe with promise. For a few years that dream held. Then feast turned into famine, followed by cyclical weather patterns and ever-changing marketing conditions beyond their control.

After a population surge in the 1910s and 1920s, people drifted away. Kidder County's residents are aging. Its population in 2000 stood at 2750. Six years later the count dropped to an estimated 2453. One quarter of its citizens are over age sixty-five, with forty-four the median age. Most grade schools have closed. The youth attend a consolidated high school, and then most leave for college and jobs in urban areas. None of my classmates remain on the farm.

Prosperity from dry-land farming in North Dakota's short growing season remains an elusive dream today. Small farmers face tough global competition. Only a few North Dakota families can support themselves on the land without outside salaries, although notable success stories exist. When the farmers move off the land, the small towns die along with that way of life.

While visiting Robinson Cemetery, I take comfort that my father, Bruce Price, now rests near his parents whom he lost so early. In death, the father I loved has joined the Price grandparents whose love I never knew.

My father and grandfather were rooted in the soil. Even with an interlude in Los Angeles, the Price family never lost faith in the promise of the land, using it as a safety net and returning to it again and again.

A few yards away in the graveyard I see the Shirley surname carved on the marble tombstone of my maternal grandparents, whom I was privileged to know and love. They too revered the land.

These two pioneer families, the Prices and the Shirleys, were members of the last generation of homesteaders in America's heartland. If only the land could tell us its story. Land is the connecting thread that weaves through three generations for a hundred years. Life on the prairie dramatically impacted each person who lived there, yet the land itself remains largely unchanged.

As a family member who left the prairie, I wonder if the land had fulfilled the dreams and visions of my grandparents and provided them with a better life. Or did it simply wring the life out of them? Did their arduous labors break the land into submission, or were they broken by it? Perhaps some of each.

The manner of life of my grandfathers and my parents is gone. I stand in awe of their tenacity. Dad was proud when his Checkerboard Farm earned the state's designation of Pioneer Farm. The land remains in the family and will soon become a Centennial Farm on the one-hundred-year anniversary of its settlement.

But what of the next hundred years? We may have come full circle with the natural rhythm of Nature. Perhaps the land will be returned to wildlife, no longer to bison, but to the migratory birds of North America which nest here. Today Kidder County is recognized as a world-class location for bird watching. Would that be dishonoring my grandparents' vision?

Life on the prairie is not the same. Technology, transportation, and a declining population have forever changed the way of life of my childhood. Those living in North Dakota today have to adapt, just as my grandparents did when they first arrived.

I am comfortable living in a metropolis; however, the place where I was born and raised is still home. No matter where I live, I feel connected to the earth. One day I will inherit a part of the farmland whose economic future is uncertain. The land that shaped me remains, and I wonder if one can really go home again. For me the answer is a literal "no." I cannot recreate my childhood era; however, I carry within my DNA my grandparents' love for the land. My rural heritage stirs in my soul.

I am and always will be a farmer's daughter.

Parents Bruce and Evelyn Price celebrated 25 years of marriage in 1968.

Grandparents Gust, Tom, and Adria each gained title to 160 acres of homestead lands.

Price Checkerboard Farm circa 1949 and 1984.
Later photo by Raymond Riskedahl.

About the Author

Judy Cook's roots inspire a compelling story of her grandparents' homesteading experiences in North Dakota. Millions flocked westward and filed for homesteads, but few remained. Her grandparents were the last generation to homestead America's heartland.

The author provides a riveting look at three generations of life on the Northern Plains where she spent her formative years. This candid and moving account portrays her four grandparents and their children carving out life on the inhospitable prairie. She offers a poignant and often entertaining glimpse into their lives. The author recounts how she grew up on the same land in the 1950s, shaped by a way of life since vanished.

Judy's maternal grandmother arrived on the prairie alone, an immigrant from Norway who learned English along with the ways of her new land. Her maternal grandfather followed a traditional agricultural path, becoming a successful grain and beef cattle farmer. Judy's paternal grandmother, born in Dakota Territory and college-educated, filed for a homestead in her own name. Non-traditional and progressive for her time, she was elected as County Superintendent of Schools before women had full voting rights. Judy's paternal grandfather lived a storied life as a farmer, cowboy, businessman, jack-of-all-trades, and Kidder County Sheriff. Moving back and forth between California and Dakota, he never lost faith in the promise of the land.

The land dramatically impacted her grandparents, but the land itself remains largely unchanged.

The author gives unique insights into a place that is simply a blank slate for most Americans. She has lived in two different worlds—rural North Dakota and suburban Los Angeles. Her story takes us back 100 years to an era when millions of our grandparents settled mid-America.

This memoir resonates for all who have pioneers in their family tree or are curious about rural life in 1900. It examines with humor and compassion the settlers' expectations, triumphs, and tragedies.

"My rural heritage stirs in my soul. I am and always will be a farmer's daughter."

The author, a graduate of the University of North Dakota, lives in Los Angeles County with her husband, Robert. Judy enjoys singing, travel, genealogy, gardening, and life in general.

Notes and Sources

General references used throughout book

Public records the author used include: Kidder County land, marriage, school, probate, and vital records; Robinson Township Vital Statistics; United States census records; vital records, atlases, census, and land records from North Dakota, South Dakota, Minnesota, Nebraska, Michigan, and California; vital, census, and church records from Canada and Norway; naturalization records; ships passenger lists; city directories; and United States military and pension records.

United States Land Patent records accessed on www.glorecords.blm.gov and in local courthouses. World War I Draft Registration Cards, 1917–1918, Kidder County, North Dakota digital images by subscription from Ancestry. com at http://www.ancestry.com. Census statistics from newspaper clippings and www.census.gov/population/cencounts/nd190090.txt.

The following history books were used extensively:
Golden Jubilee, Robinson, North Dakota 1911–1961;
Diamond Jubilee History, Robinson, North Dakota 1911–1986;
Diamond Jubilee, 1881–1956, Steele, N. Dak. (Mandan, ND: Crescent Printing Co.);
Dawson Centennial 1880–1980, the First 100 Years;
History of Richland County, 1977, Richland County Historical Society;
Charles Pinkney, *Early History of Fairmount, Souvenir Edition* (Fairmount, ND: R.A. Fairmount Publishing Co).

References about the state and the climate include:

The Compiled Laws of the State of North Dakota, 1913, and Supplement to the 1913 Compiled Laws of North Dakota, 1913-1925, from State Historical Society of North Dakota.

Larry Remele, State Historical Society of North Dakota, *North Dakota History: Overview and Summary,* North Dakota, 1988. Accessed at http://www.nd.gov/hist/ndhist.htm

http://www.nd.gov/hist/chrono.html

http://ngeorgia.com/weather/gainesvilletornado.html

http://www.prairiepublic.org/programs/datebook/bydate/06/0706/070606.jsp

Newspaper accounts came from clippings in author's collection, digitized archive microfilm, or Ancestry.com subscription databases. Newspaper archives used on loan from the North Dakota Historical Society include: *Robinson Times* microfilm roll 3507–Aug 12, 1915 to Oct 10, 1918; roll 3559–Feb 4, 1915 to Aug 5, 1915. *Steele Ozone* roll 1675–Jul 21, 1911 to Dec 2, 1915; roll 1676–Dec 2, 1915, to Feb 13, 1919; roll 1677–Feb 13, 1919 to Jun 22, 1922; roll 1678–Jun 22, 1922 to Jun 4, 1925; and roll 1679–Jun 4, 1925 to May 24, 1928.

Additional family information was gleaned from Bible records, funeral cards, obituaries, certificates of birth, death, marriage, and baptism, financial records, medical records, family letters, and photographs. Interviews with seniors who remembered my grandparents, especially Mary White (age 99), proved invaluable.

Chapter References

THE LAND IN THE BEGINNING

http://survey.swc.nd.gov/

Fargo Forum, Fargo, ND, Aug 5, 1951: Reprinted in *Steele Ozone*, Steele, ND, Jun 14, 1956, "Killing of Dr. Weiser Touches Off Fight with Sioux North of Tappen."

Steele Ozone, Steele, ND, Sep 18, 1974, "Monument Dedicated to Those Who Each Thought They Were Right," p. 2.

Harper's Weekly, Sep 12, 1863. http://www.sonofthesouth.net/leefoundation/civil-war/1863/september/sibley-sioux-indian-expedition.htm

Oscar Garrett Wall, *Recollections of the Sioux Massacre. An Authentic History of the Yellow Medicine Incident, of the Fate of Marsh and his Men, of the Siege and Battles of Fort Ridgely, and of Other Important Battles and Experiences. Together with a Historical Sketch of the Sibley Expedition of 1863*, The Home Printery, M. C. Russell, Prop'r. 1909. Author's copy.

PRAIRIE JUSTICE

Kidder County Jail Register 1899–1920, pages 4–6, copied in courthouse, Steele, ND. Register provides date, name, description, offense, sentence and/or discharge and remarks and list of county sheriffs.

Steele Ozone, "T.E. Glass & Daughter of Dawson, Murdered" Oct 31, 1912.

Steele Ozone, "Geo. Baker, Slayer of Father-in-law & Wife, is Victim" Nov 14, 1912.

SUPERVISING SCHOOLMARMS

The Legacy of North Dakota's Country Schools, Warren A. Henke and Everett
C. Albers, Editors (Bismarck: North Dakota Humanities Council,
Inc., 1998), p. 256. Used with permission.

The Legacy of North Dakota's Country Schools, previously cited, p. 251. Used
with permission.

Robinson Times, Robinson, ND, Oct 1916, paid political announcements.

Superintendent of Public Instruction Acct 77–5–4 (pt. 3) Dept of County
Superintendent, Vol. 45 1916–17 Pt. 1 (Adams–McLean. P. 3–25
and Vol. 43 pages 2, 3, 21, 24, and 25.

Annual reports submitted by County Superintendent accessed by author
at State Historical Society in Bismarck, North Dakota, especially,
"Report of County Superintendent of Schools, County of Kidder,
State of North Dakota, for year ending June 30, 1917."

A LIFE-CHANGING MOMENT UNDER THE BIG TOP

Lorraine Sommerfeld, "The Show Must Go On," *North Dakota Horizons,*
Summer 1994, p. 7.

The Farmer-Globe, Aug 15, 1966, p. 1, "Circus Visit Here Recalls Tragedy of
69 Years Ago."

Fargo Forum, "Shattered Tent Pole in Stone Recalls Wahpeton Circus Tragedy
63 Years Ago."

"Wahpeton's Famous Monument," Anonymous article, undated, accessed in
Leach Public Library in Wahpeton, ND.

"Big Top Tragedy," undated, unnamed newspaper clipping in author's
collection.

FEUD TURNS TO MURDER

Bismarck Tribune, Bismarck, ND, Dec 21, 1916, p. 1; Jul 9, 1917, p. 1; Jul
12, 1917, p. 9.

Author's undated newspaper clippings.

GUNDER AND MAREN SJØLI, MATERNAL GREAT-GRANDPARENTS: NORWEGIANS COME TO AMERICA

"The Sjolie Family Reunion of 1980, Gunder and Maren Sjolie, Rothsay,
Minnesota" compilation, Robinson, North Dakota, Jun 28 and 29,
1980. Author's copy.

"Shirley Family Reunion" compilation, Robinson, North Dakota, Jul 4, 1986. Author's copy.

"Shirley Family Reunion" compilation, Aug 1994. Author's copy.

Gloria Radtke, "Appreciation for My Heritage." *Reaching the Millennium: Events and Inventions That Changed Our Lives,* compilation, Otter Tail County Historical Society, Fergus Falls, MN (Fergus Falls, MN: Annika Publications, 1999). Author's copy.

Petra Hanson, Maternal Grandmother: Babies and Baking

Mildred Hanson, "My Autobiography" circa 1976. Author's copy.

Gabriel Lundy, "Brief Family History, Pertaining to Parents, Sisters, and Brothers, Aunts, Uncles, Cousins and Ancestors" Jul 1956. Author's copy.

Gloria Radtke, "Appreciation for My Heritage" previously cited.

Author's original papers of Petra's voyage.

Oil!

Bill Shemorry, "Robinson oil well: Was it a dry hole?" *Williston Basin Oil Reporter*, Oct 27, 1983, Williston, ND.

Forlorn February Funeral

Steele Ozone, "Death of Mrs. Thomas Price" [notice] Feb 20, 1936, and "Mrs. T. A. Price" [obituary] Feb 27, 1936.

A Life's Work

Inventory and Bill of Sale from Thomas Price's probate papers, Kidder County Courthouse, Steele, ND. Author's copies.

Steele Ozone, "Last Rites Held for Tom Price" Feb 23, 1939.

Great-Grandpa Daniel's Adventures

"*History of Tuscola County, Biographical Sketches and Illustrations, Elmwood Biographies 1883*" (Chicago: H. R. Page Co., 1883). Accessed on USGenWeb Archives.

MANHUNT

Bismarck Tribune, Jun 25, 1973, p.1; Jun 26, 1973, p.1; Jun 27, 1973, p.1;
    Jun 28, 1973, p.1.
Steele Ozone-Press, Jun 27, 1973, p. 1, Jul 4, 1973, p.1.
The Forum, Fargo-Moorhead, Jun 26, 1973, p.1.

CIRCLE OF LIFE

Chris Santella and Bill Thompson, "*Fifty Places to Go Birding Before You Die,
    Birding Experts Share the World's Greatest Destinations*" (New York:
    Stewart, Tabori, and Chang, Inc., 2007).

About the Cover Photo

Keg Party. Carl Wick of Robinson, North Dakota, far right, took the cover photograph. He activated his camera with a string.

From left, standing: Carl Shirley, Oscar Madson, Andrew Stephenson, John Vallin, Tom Nelson, unidentified boy, Harry Nelson, Gust Stenberg; Seated: Pete Konningrud, Tom Price, Ed Hermanson, Carl Wick.

The dozen neighbors, posing about 1910, look confident, if not cocky. In the prosperous early years of settlement, anything seemed possible. Life was good. Optimism reigned on the prairie after an abundant wheat harvest, yet many pioneers were destined to fail on the semi-arid land.

The author's grandfather, Tom Price, extends his hand on the spigot tap of the ten-gallon keg. The photo pre-dates Tom's election as county sheriff, at which time he was sworn to enforce, but not necessarily agree with, the state prohibition laws.

Printed in the United States
127560LV00003B/43-102/P